MW01379510

SECRET HISTORIES

STORIES OF COURAGE, RISK, AND REVELATION

Edited by: Brenda Peterson, Laura Foreman, Meredith Bailey

The Salish Sea Writers is a private Seattle-based community. Its members meet to share their stories, hone their writing skills, and review and comment on one another's in-progress works of nonfiction, fiction, and poetry. Author Brenda Peterson is the group's *sensei*, teaching invaluable lessons about the art and craft of writing, as well as the realities of contemporary publishing.

Most of the stories collected in *Secret Histories* were developed in the course of working together. Where pieces have been previously published, publication details are placed at the end of the story. All publisher permissions for reprint have been secured. Each author holds exclusive rights to his or her contribution to this collection and is solely responsible for the contents of his or her story.

ISBN: 0615904300
ISBN-13: 9780615904306
Library of Congress Control Number: 2013920009
CreateSpace Independent Publishing Platform
North Charleston, South Carolina

Cover design by Elizabeth M. Watson

"Your visions will become clear only when you can look into your own heart. Who looks outside, dreams; who looks inside, awakes."

- *C.G. Jung*

CONTENTS

ACKNOWLEDGMENTS

INTRODUCTION
Brenda Peterson

COURAGE

RISK

REVELATION

AUTHOR BIOGRAPHIES

ACKNOWLEDGMENTS

Though writing requires periods of great solitude, a book is never a solitary journey. It takes a community to create an anthology. We want to gratefully acknowledge Susan Bloch and the delicious Indian dinner she served us in her home, for it was there that *Secret Histories: Stories of Courage, Risk, and Revelation* began.

Without the professional expertise, organization, and infinite patience of Wendy Noritake, *Secret Histories* might never have become more than a dream. Her vision as creative director and her skills in project and production management have been critical in transforming this book into a reality.

We also want to thank our editorial board: Laura Foreman, Lindsay Pyfer, Margie Combs, Amanda Mander, Lizbeth Adams, and Tess Williams. Somehow they found time in their busy-to-capacity lives to carefully read and edit each story, supporting the work of our lead editors: Brenda Peterson, Meredith Bailey, and Laura Foreman.

A book that isn't marketed goes nowhere, and so we also thank our marketing team: Amanda Mander, Elizabeth Van Deventer, Kathy Opie, and Laura Foreman. Again, Wendy Noritake stepped up and, drawing on her years of experience, guided and provided us with the marketing strategy and planning. With great savvy, the team tackled everything from social media to social events—all in service of getting our beloved book out into the world.

The old adage says "never judge a book by its cover," but in this case, the creative genius of Elizabeth Watson produced a truly elegant cover design that was cheered by all as it somehow magically represented every story in *Secret Histories*. Coupled with the point-on flap copy written by Marlene Blessing, any potential reader can indeed favorably judge this book by its cover.

There are those who have answered the call: from legal advice to proofreading. We thank Margie Combs, Amanda Mander, John Runyan, Susan Little, Kip Greenthal, Donna James, and Lindsay Pyfer.

Finally, we must give thanks to Brenda Peterson, a truly wise woman. Inspired by her beloved Salish Sea, she has generously created and guided a writing community that, like water, is soft and yielding, yet strong and powerful.

INTRODUCTION

Secret Histories, Shared Stories

The authors in this collection enjoy the nourishing, yet rigorous, scrutiny of a creative community of working writers—all deeply engaged in the practice and art of sharing stories. Here, you'll discover memoir, fiction, poetry, and even excerpts from novels-in-progress. You'll step into lives and stories that may be wildly different from yours or mirror your own. This book is a rich mix of cultures, travelers, and voices. But one thing these pieces have in common is that their authors show up on the page.

It takes true *courage* to reveal yourself or your history. When seventy-year-old Mary-san bravely broke her culture's reticence and wrote a memoir of her years in the World War II internment camps, *Looking Like the Enemy* was a bestseller. Mary, at eighty-eight, has just published her third book, *Becoming Mama-san: 80 Years of Wisdom*. Read her story, "The Last Dance in the Searchlight," and remember what Mary-san told National Public Radio, "Please, don't let it happen—*again*."

Courage must always be summoned when facing racism, like Susan Little's Emma McGee in America's Deep South or the African slave, Gabriel, who secretly practices his Yoruba faith in "Calling Forth." In "The Horn of Africa," a devoted nurse works with Somali women to ease an ancient ritual. Sometimes courage is about letting go and simply witnessing, as in the elegiac, "For Children Who Lost Fathers to the Sea," or saying goodbye to a beloved animal in "Violet" and "Passages."

It's a real *risk* to tell your secrets, even more so when they've been long hidden and denied. Whether it's a favorite teacher in "Rumour of Red" who chides an adoring student for wearing bright lipstick; a therapist who stands up at a memorial service to speak "The Unspeakable"; an abiding sister whose homeless brother is lost and wandering; a mother who witnesses her daughter's tattoo and unveils a family secret; a Bernese mountain dog who calms a troubled family; a South African maid who embodies compassion and loyalty even amidst the "Eyes Shut" of apartheid; or a sister growing up with an autistic brother in "Cracker Jacks," who discovers the dark, compassionate light of humor.

For the reader, *revelation* or epiphany is the real gift. It's what we read to uncover our own lives and stories. Crafting an epiphany is like skillfully building wings—so that the reader may soar with us and see the wide landscape in light and shadow. Sometimes this perspective, which I call "the mature narrator," offers a glimpse of wisdom that can only come when we travel outside of our own closed sets—family, country, and culture.

Many of the stories in this Revelation section travel inward *and* outward. In "A Shift in Vision," an art student glimpses wings in a painting that lift her out of "negative space." In Harvard Yard, during a 1960s protest, a young student changes the course of his personal history. A niece searches for the truth about a Japanese-American soldier's death in "Finding Uncle Yosh." A young nurse travelling to Nepal glimpses the gift of introspection in "Alone, Not Lonely." A secretive Italian immigrant lies to tell the truth of her Old World in "Tell Me a Story," and in "Out of the Ether," the epiphany actually comes from out of this world.

As mentor to the remarkable community of writers in this anthology, I've taught and been taught by them. Some of these writers have read and critiqued each other for years—through divorces, illnesses, triumphs, and sabbaticals. Our weekly critique has strengthened and refined their skills; it has also drawn us closer. While we focus on craft, a sense of shared purpose and knowing each other's lives and work also buoys us. Our intent is to help each other in the fiercely honest and hopeful goal of growing together—as writers.

This community has launched individual books and many of the writers frequently publish their work in literary magazines and other journals. In an age of indie publishing, these writers wanted to learn about bookmaking together. Our editorial board reached out to professional editors, book designers, and production managers.

Writing can be a solitary and competitive business. But in our community, writers can take quantum leaps, knowing they have mentoring, encouragement, and abiding support. This anthology is a leap. We hope you'll take wing with us into *Secret Histories*. Just open the door.

- Brenda Peterson

COURAGE

Life shrinks or expands in proportion to one's courage.

– Anais Nin

HITCHHIKING

By: Kimberly S. Richardson

"Aikido is the spirit of loving protection for all beings, including our attackers."

– O Sensei

On a hazy winter afternoon, a dead car battery left me flagging down a ride in West Seattle, Washington. At thirty-five years old, I knew hitchhiking was dangerous, but I had to get to work. It was 1990, a time before cell phones and, in my haste, I didn't stop to consider other options for transportation. Impatiently, I stood just off the curb, stuck my thumb out, and, after several minutes, a man in a dingy blue sedan pulled over.

"I need to get to the Chevron station just a mile down the road," I said, relieved to be on my way as I jumped in the front seat. Instantly, I felt the slimy squish of ketchup wrappers under my feet. When I looked down, I saw a sea of Big Mac containers carpeting the floor.

"Okay," he muttered.

I noticed his round balding head, slumped shoulders, and big belly. He looked downtrodden. Had I been more alert, I might have perceived that something was wrong when I got into the vehicle, but I was in a hurry to cross the bridge before traffic jammed up. Then, the car in front of us began to slow down and wander across the yellow line.

From out of nowhere, he started to rant. "Lady," he spat. "Who gave you a driver's license?" I wanted to ask how he could tell that the driver was a woman, but thought better of it. That's when the rancid smell of mildew hit my nostrils. Out of the corner of my eye, I noticed the wadded up bags of clothes piled high in the back seat. *Did he live out of his car?*

"Fuckin' women. Nothing is ever right with them. Bitches, all of them."

Alarm bells went off in my head, and I stretched the muscles of my neck to feel a little taller. He continued facing straight ahead, never looking at me. We neared the gas station. I wanted to get my feet back on the ground.

"My stop is coming up on the left here. You can just pull over and I'll let myself out."

As I stole sideways glances at him, thoughts of the Green River Killer sent a cold shiver up my spine. Recently, there had been a series of articles in *The Seattle Times* charting his menacing history of murdering more than fifty women in the Northwest. I didn't want to be paranoid, but I needed to get out of that car.

For the first time, he looked at me. Dirt clung to the pores in his gray skin. His overcoat needed a stitch where the sleeve met the shoulder. "Shut up. I'll tell you when your stop is coming up."

At that moment, I was beginning to hope that the twelve years of training in the martial art of aikido would assist me in dealing with what could be a dangerous encounter. "It's right here on the left," I announced as resolutely as I could.

"Do you need me to shut you up?"

Suddenly, it all came back. My body shuddered as the buried memory burst to life. In a flash, I could see Lisa's bright reflection flicker through the windshield like a lantern glow. She had been a perfect match in friendship. A Bronx-born girl, she had moon-shaped eyes, long, thick chestnut hair, and always a pair of bright red Keds on her feet. We met in the year between high school and college in eastern Massachusetts. When I shared her company, I felt as though I could be someone I had not yet imagined possible. Watching her reinvent herself each day both inspired and taunted me to forget my own timidity. I became fearless and could speak my mind with ease when in her company. As roommates, we spent many evenings together swapping life stories.

One winter night, she hitchhiked a ride home and was found the next morning one hundred feet down an embankment. She'd been bludgeoned to death. I didn't know Lisa's plans that particular evening. She had a boyfriend and would sometimes spend the night with him, so I wasn't worried when she didn't make it home. Months later, when the murderer told his story at the trial, he commented that her feisty temperament aroused him. He wanted her and the fight in her. The attitude that I loved infuriated him. When she had exited the moving vehicle, he turned his car around and hunted her down.

"She got what she deserved," her murderer had mouthed defiantly.

After Lisa died, I refused to think about her or talk about her. It was just too painful. It never occurred to me to connect my aikido practice to her death. Honestly, given how hopeless I felt about the gruesome circumstances of her passing, I made an unconscious pact with myself to keep her locked away in the back of my mind. It had been my dead place, until that moment.

The car's abrupt acceleration tore me out of remembering and plunged me into the realization that something just as awful could be in store for me. By now, we had passed the gas station and were headed out of town.

Study your options. I coached myself as if I were training at the dojo. I could open the passenger door and take a roll, but the car was going forty miles per hour. Not the best choice. I knew that if I moved with the right amount of speed and precision, I could wrap the palm of my hand around the back of his neck, jam my thumb into his carotid artery, and stop the flow of blood to his brain. But immobilizing the driver in a moving vehicle also seemed like a risky plan. Better to consider what I studied daily: that focused awareness—an unperturbed mind, not brute strength—is the key to handling jeopardy.

I considered a third alternative: Appeal to his humanity. How many times during my years as a psychotherapist had I witnessed grief and rage with court-ordered, anger-management clients? Doing intakes eight hours a day required that I stay clear and calm as I listened to their turbulent stories. I had to figure out a way of applying some of that focus here if I wanted to get out of this car alive and unharmed.

"You don't sound happy," I ventured.

Incoherent grumbling sounds poured out of his mouth. Then, "You think I'm pissed? My wife split and took the kids with her. No note, no nothing. Don't know where she went. What am I 'sposed to do? Goddamn bitch." He paused and looked at me again. "Every one of you. Every. One. Of. You." He made an odd gurgling sound in his throat.

"That's awful. It must really hurt." I could feel the sweat pouring from my armpits and dripping down my rib cage. *Keep it together, girl.*

"You're all the same. Just walk out, leave a mess," he replied. Moisture pooled above his top lip and his hands tightly gripped the steering wheel. Then he said darkly, menacingly, "Maybe I should mess with you . . . "

Breathe now. "I know you're mad. But I know . . . and you know, that it wasn't me who hurt you." I was careful to pronounce every word slowly and clearly. "And I know that it's not me you want to hurt."

It was growing dark. I could see the twinkling lights of the boats gliding across Puget Sound on the right side of me and the bungalow-style houses along Alki Avenue on the left. The houses seemed so close, the people inside within arm's reach, yet they might as well have been on another continent for all the good they could do. I concentrated hard now: feet on the floorboard, tailbone anchored on the threadbare seat. What did I have to lose by trying to shift his mind away from me? Here was the moment where the situation could change. If he didn't start seeing me as a human being, things were going to go really badly. Hour after hour on the Aikido mat, I had practiced connecting to the human heart in my attacker. Maybe it would work now.

You're not really interested in hurting me. "If you gave it any thought at all—you'd want to let me out on the side of the road now," I offered softly. "If not for me, then for you." Out of the corner of my eye, I could see his hands clenched on the wheel. His jaw tightened down as though cinched in a vice. Moments passed, though it seemed more like hours. It felt like all the air in the car was being siphoned off. Offering no response, he pressed his foot deeper into the accelerator and we sailed down the road. *Give it one more shot.* I took a deep breath. As gently as possible, I said again, "You can pull over now."

Something clicked in him. He slammed his foot on the brake and leaned his chest on the steering wheel. The car pitched forward and stopped.

"Get the fuck out!" he snarled.

Fireworks went off in my head.

Move now. Don't think. Don't look back.

I jumped out quickly. As the car sped away, sweat rained down my chest. Tiny hammers pounded nails inside my head. My thoughts streamed:

He was going to kill me.

Where am I?

Have to teach at six.

Oh my God.

He didn't hurt me.

I didn't hurt him.

It was a long walk to the gas station, and, like Walter Mitty, I was a short distance from my body the whole way. I was so shaken up, I didn't even get his license plate—big error. When I reached the gas station, I did think twice before getting in the attendant's truck, but his sincere wish to help felt real. He gave me a ride to my own car and charged the battery.

Once in my car, my body began to shake like a rattle. I was both ecstatic to be alive and still terrified. *You got in that car without once looking at that guy. Awareness, girl, how could you forget about awareness? And how could you have forgotten about Lisa?*

I arrived late to the dojo that evening to teach. A radiant fire blazed through my body when I stepped on the mat. The moment that my student raced toward me, intent to strike, I could see the whole interaction in slow motion. By the time he was in range to deliver a blow, I'd shifted slightly off to the side and slipped behind him. With my hand firmly wrapped around his neck, I used his own momentum to lift him off his feet. I knew in that moment I could apply just the right amount of force to either neutralize his attack or break his neck. How similar this moment was to my experience with the stranger in the car just hours ago. How closely juxtaposed are the touches that protect and the touches that destroy. Effortlessly, I guided my student to the ground.

As I locked the dojo door after class and stepped into the street, a light rain began to fall. Finally, fully free to think, I asked questions like a mantra: *What if he hadn't stopped? What if I had ended up like Lisa? Why did he finally pull over?*

Now I had fully embodied that lesson I hadn't learned when Lisa was murdered: Everything can change in a moment. That harrowing car ride unwound a knot wedged deep in me. For all my years of practicing martial arts to face my fears, out of nowhere, I tumbled into a place that I had never resolved—the anguish of Lisa's senseless death. I couldn't have imagined that a fifteen-minute ride would force me to revisit her memory and acutely face my own vulnerability.

As I turned the key in the ignition of my car and flipped on the headlights, tears streamed down my face. I realized my decision to reach for reason over violence had just saved my life. What I learned then is still true for me so many years later. Effective self-defense is not about punching or striking. It's about cultivating deep personal power, vivid self-awareness, and reaching for the truth, in others, even when you aren't sure of the outcome. My interaction with the foul-smelling, despondent human being in that car forever changed the way I looked at martial arts. I can only hope that as he drove down the road, angry and bereft of his family, that maybe in some small way I changed him, too. Perhaps, at least for one moment, he knew compassion.

FOR CHILDREN WHO LOST FATHERS TO THE SEA

By: Janet McLain Smith

Did they believe we did not know,
like blind children lost
to the crossings of monkey bars, cold
to the touch from too much
sea and winter?

Moving like ancient oceans,
did they think we could not see
through our gray playing, singing,
swinging? Could not feel our mothers
move en masse when thick fogs dropped,
ferries crashed, and shrill blasts shouted
a life, one of our own, was lost?

We always stopped,
like statues frozen by a game of tag,
to listen to the running of frightened men,
their metal pails clanging, to feel the dark
tide of women move into their bellies
praying that the capsized, the broken,
was not all that remained.

The gulls riding the tides with their woeful
screams were too busy fishing for ice-blue herring
to notice that it was one of our fathers
whose face was now one with the bottom fish.

Maybe they had to believe the one safe place
in our town, besides the plots and lines and crosses
marking the final resting place of those we loved
most, was the playground, where little minds were so lost
to worlds of madhatters, that we could not know
the truth that found and chilled even a child's blood.

PASSAGES

By: Clare Hodgson Meeker

We were stopped at a roadside restaurant off I-5 on the way to take our daughter to college when I got the call that our eleven-year-old dog was dying. "Chaser has stopped eating," said my friend, her voice low and concerned.

I walked outside with the cell phone to my ear. "Did you call the vet?" I shouted, barely able to hear myself over the roaring traffic.

The naturopathic vet had been my saving grace these past few months since our sheltie was diagnosed with kidney failure. She showed me how to give Chaser daily intravenous injections to flush the toxins out of his system. Chaser would stand patiently as I fumbled with the thick fold of skin behind his collar and pushed the needle in. I was never comfortable doing it, but the treatment seemed to work. He still took daily walks and perked up whenever he smelled food. Before this trip, I had asked the vet how long this treatment might continue to work. The vet's parting words came back to me now. "He'll let you know when it's time."

Standing by the edge of the freeway, I tried to figure out what to do. Here we were ushering our daughter into her new life. If I flew back to Seattle now to be with Chaser, I would not see her dorm room or meet her roommate. How would I know that she was safely settled if I missed this farewell ritual? Would my daughter think I was choosing Chaser over her?

The vinyl seat squeaked as I sat down in the restaurant booth next to my husband. "Chaser's stopped eating," I said, ignoring the coleslaw that had just arrived.

"Not even carrots?" asked my son between bites of food. Chaser loved carrots—a welcome treat from his dry dog food diet. He would lie down, position the carrot straight up between his paws, and slowly nibble it down to the nub. I'm sure it was carrots that made his white and sable coat shine.

"You should eat something," said my husband, pushing a plate with a Reuben sandwich closer to me.

"I'm not hungry," I said. "I think that Chaser may not make it until we get back. I'm not sure what to do."

"You should go home, Mom. You don't want Chaser to die when you're not there." My curly-haired, down-to-earth daughter, Sarah, was never one to beat around the bush. She could read my feelings like they were her own and express them with a boldness I could not muster. Our relationship had become strained this year as she flexed her verbal muscles in her quest for independence. After these last stormy months of her living at home, I was looking forward to having calm in the house with a guilty sense of relief. But when it came to Chaser, there were no fragile egos to protect, only one sweet dog we both loved.

Chaser came into our lives eleven years ago. We chose the runt of the litter, passing up the bigger, noisier puppies that begged for attention for the one with the delicate, foxlike features and deep, brown eyes. The breeder called him "Homeboy" because she said he rarely left her side. But from the moment I reached out my hand for him to gently sniff, he seemed to be comfortable with us.

I wanted my kids to experience that bond with an animal, the way I had felt growing up with our Labrador retriever, Babe. Babe was gentle and steadfastly devoted to our family. She patiently endured my climbing on her back during my horse-loving phase, and protected me when I floated out the door in my pajamas one night, fully asleep. According to my parents, she followed me down the driveway, blocking my path so I would not cross the street, and barked until my parents retrieved me.

The instinct to protect was strong in Chaser, too. At first, my kids were frightened when he nipped at their heels as they ran around the backyard with him. I explained to them that he was simply doing the job shelties were bred to do: herding them in line to keep them out of harm's way. Once they understood his behavior, they were no longer afraid. My son named him Chaser, and from that day on, whenever Chaser got excited, the kids would obediently stop running and wait for him to come over and lick their hands.

In what seemed like no time at all, the children grew busy with their own lives, leaving Chaser and me to look after each other. Standing at attention by my desk, he would remind me when it was time to take a break from writing and get some exercise. And when I could not take him with me, he would settle into a shallow hole he had dug in the dirt next to the front door to wait until I returned. Chaser guarded his territory with a keen eye for strangers. Neither big dogs nor noisy garbage collectors were exempt from suspicion when it came to protecting his family.

Now, as I waved goodbye to my family at the airport in Sacramento, I wondered what kind of comfort and protection I could give Chaser in this last phase of his life. When my friend picked me up at the airport, Chaser stood up to greet me, even though his legs were trembling. I felt a sudden hopefulness in this simple act of devotion. Would he rally one more time for me?

What makes dogs show such loyalty to their human companions? Like the fierce, protective love between a parent and child, it is hard to parse instinct from emotion. But I believe dogs possess superior powers to empathize and act on their feelings when a situation presents itself. They show us how to be more humane. The vet once called Chaser an old soul. "We all have something to learn from him," she said.

That night, Chaser did not touch his food or water. He lay down next to my bed in his usual place, but I lifted him onto the bed with me. I told him stories about our life together, laughing and tearing up at times. I asked him if he remembered his one act of teenage rebellion when he ran away from home, scaring us half to death until a neighbor brought him back. Chaser's mouth opened the way a dog smiles.

The next morning, I drove with him to the park, and we sat down in the grass. A dog barked and Chaser's ears shot up. In the past, my fearless protector would have chased the other dog away. But this time, Chaser did not get up. He just looked at me. What was the point in living, his eyes seemed to say, if he could not act on the herding instinct that was his pride and joy. He was telling me it was time.

That day, I made an appointment with the vet. My whole body was trembling. The shot was quick and Chaser did not flinch. As his breathing slowed, I leaned my face against his and told him that I loved him one last time.

For weeks after his passing, I could not stop crying. My friends assumed that it was my daughter's leaving that had made me such an emotional wreck. But here I was about to turn fifty and had never experienced the death of someone this close to me before.

The truth was that I missed them both. The house was too quiet now. Sarah called and asked me how I was doing. I could tell from her tone of voice that she was worried about me. "Maybe you should talk with the vet," she said. "She might have some good advice for you."

The idea of asking an animal specialist to solve my problem seemed strangely comforting. Walking into the vet's office brought a new flood of tears. "It feels like I've contracted some strange disease," I told her. "Will I ever feel normal again?"

The vet looked at me and smiled. Her dark eyes, like Chaser's, drew me gently in. "You know, I think Chaser's spirit is still in this world. He's just waiting to make sure that you're okay," she said.

I was humbled by the thought that Chaser might still be trying to protect me. After weeks of crying and sleepwalking through my days, I knew in that moment that I was strong enough to let him go. I did not want to hold Chaser back from his next great adventure. Nor did I want to distract my daughter from focusing on her new life. Letting them move on would not change either relationship. Sarah and I would continue to talk. She would soon be coming home for Thanksgiving, and Chaser would always be watching out for us.

VIOLET

By: Catherine Johnson

"I'll do the pigs first," John said, reaching for his rifle. Behind us, the mobile butcher truck idled, a low humming sound in the early morning cold. "Who'll get the gate?" he asked.

"I will," I said.

Slaughter day at the farm was always hard, like the late November ground on which it occurred. Each autumn, the lambs that we had labored to bring into the world the previous spring, we soberly ushered out. In a matter of hours, the fields that had abounded all summer with their life were frozen into a wintery silence. This year was no different, and yet very different. This year, for the first time, we had raised a couple of pigs along with the sheep.

John and I stepped into the barn, our presence startling some of the lambs. We waited while they resettled. It is important to minimize any stress the animals feel since stress affects the quality and taste of meat.

"Good lookin' bunch this year," John said softly, referring to both the numbers in the flock, as well as their size.

"Yeah. They are." I couldn't think of anything else to say. All I knew was that I wanted to get this over with. We started toward the stalls where the pigs slept, crossing through a dusty shaft of sunlight streaming through a crack in the east wall.

When the pigs were just plump little shoats, we discovered they were late sleepers. Early each morning when we fed the sheep, the pigs would rouse for their breakfast too, but quickly return to their stalls for a little more shuteye.

John and I reached the gate to Violet's stall. She was, as I had imagined, still sleeping, lying on her side. Violet was an enormous white Yorkshire pig with an equally enormous personality. While the lambs were uneasy around us, the pigs seemed to enjoy our company and none more than Violet. I reached for her gate as time ticked to a stop.

I remember John's presence beside me, the feel of rough barn wood in my hands and then the cold hard metal of the gate's latch. I remember how my heart began slowing, slowing, slowing as I slid that latch quietly back. All sound seemed muted, the way it does in fog or falling snow.

Violet stirred, shifted her weight, rolled from her side a little more upright, and opened her eyes. I met her gaze but I could not hold it. I think she knew something was different about that morning. Her eyes, normally bright and curious, looked dark and sad. The latch reached its stop point with a soft click.

I have eaten meat all my life. Part of my coming to live and work on this farm was to answer, for myself, whether the killing of animals for food was something I could live with—not only live with but be present to and participate in. If I was going to eat meat, then shouldn't I be willing to take part in the killing?

Quietly, I opened the gate. John stepped beside me, raised his rifle, and fired. The life flowed out of Violet. Her legs thrashed as nerves fired uselessly. It wrenched me to watch, but I refused to look away. It only lasted a minute, and then Violet was dead.

Violet, the pig who would raise her rooting snout when she heard us call from across the field, who would snort and grunt and break into a full-on sprint to greet us, all 350 pounds of her running on high-heeled hooves. Violet who, with inexplicable precision, would skid to a stop at the moment she reached our feet, lower her great self to the ground, roll onto her side and offer us her soft bacon belly for a tummy rub. There would be other pigs, but never again would there be a Violet.

What leads us to bond more closely with some animals while barely at all with others? Is it possible some animals choose to bond with us? All I know is our relationship with Violet was wholly personal and reciprocal.

Two weeks after the slaughter, we sat down to a dinner of pork roast. As we took our places at the table, we fell into a solemn silence. I was not the only one crying. Everyone at the farm had loved Violet, and that night all of us ate our dinner with a depth of gratitude rarely felt.

Now three years later, I realize that I have still not answered my questions about eating meat. Instead, I live with them. There are times when

I sit down to a meal with friends where I feel as if I carry a secret. Modern processing methods and packaging discourages us from considering that the chicken breast, lamb chop, or pork roast before us was once a living breathing being that someone assisted in birth, raised, and cared for daily and then, when the time came, killed. I was raised Catholic and attended Mass almost every day of my young life. Over and over, I heard the words: "This is my body, which shall be given up for you, eat this in memory of me." I know now, because of Violet, the true gift of such sacrifice.

EMMA McGEE AND THE BLUE BOTTLE TREE

By: Susan Little

Every Friday at noon, a man in a Ford pickup backs down a short gravel road to its end, empties the truck's contents onto the ground, and sets the pile on fire—that's what they do with garbage in Burton, Arkansas, in 1950. Then he drives his truck up the gravel road and out onto Highway 149 as the stench and smoke of the blaze billow behind him. At six o'clock, Emma McGee is walking over the still-warm pile, poking and prodding, excavating treasures from the town's smoldering detritus. In one hand, she holds a crooked staff reserved for this purpose, in the other, the hem of her long white satin dress.

Everyone in Burton, black and white, thinks she is two yards short of a load for wearing heavy satin dresses in the stifling heat of the Arkansas summer. But twenty years ago, when Emma McGee was born again, the Lord specifically instructed her to cover herself. In all that time, the dresses have been a measure of her turn-away from a life of sin—an outward sign of the saving grace inside her. Against white satin, the lustrous skin of Emma's African slave grandmother glows mahogany where it stretches taut over the chiseled cheekbones of her Cherokee mother. Her black eyes gleam when she talks, and her long, tapered fingers and pink palms wave gracefully, animating her speech. She is six feet tall, an apparition, the fabric flowing in the breeze of her confident strides. The whole town knows that Emma truly is what she calls "sanctified." And, until this day, there has never been a whisper of doubt.

In the early 1940s, using her own hands and scrounged materials—leftover roofing and broken sheets of plywood—Emma built herself a house at the end of this gravel road. That was long before the dump was created. But now that it is there, practically in her front yard, she has claimed it. Today, she hopes for something special: something like the salt and pepper set shaped like a pair of Chinese children in chartreuse pajamas that she found a couple of months ago. At the very least, she is certain, there will be one or two good M. O. bottles—the greatest find of all.

Blue glass bottles. Whenever Emma finds one, she washes it out in the kitchen and slides it over the tip of a bare branch on a leafless maple tree that stands between her front door and the gravel driveway to the dump. She is glad that the tree died young from lack of water—it is just the right size for a bottle tree. Glad, too, that white folks drink so much Milk of Magnesia to relieve the constipation that provides the precious bottles. In her heart, though she has never heard the phrase, Emma knows that her tree is an objet d'art. It has its own spare beauty—cobalt blue glass, arranged upon bleached-white branches, balanced and organized by nature— and its own strong history, delicately preserved from Hoodoo precedents unknown to Emma.

Poke, poke, prod, prod: Her search today reveals nothing. Emma is ready to abandon the hunt. Then, she sees something she recognizes, tucked under a broken chair leg, almost unnoticed—a sooty linen handkerchief—something she herself has washed and ironed, or ones like it. Emma drops her stick and bends over. She retrieves it in one hand and, with the other, peels back the edges of the white square to reveal, incredibly, a man's diamond ring. A wide gold band with a large and perfect blue-white stone of great value.

"Lord Jesus, help me!" she beseeches. She emits a low whistle and then another "Lord, Lord."

Emma knows this ring. It is highly prized by the Pettit family, the white people for whom she has worked for twenty-five years. The family where she has cooked and cleaned, whose children she raised and loved, especially the little one, the baby. Baby Clay. When Baby Clay married and set up his own household, he took Emma with him—to her delight. And there she has stayed, laboring and loving until this very day. Baby Clay's wife, Miz Eleanor, and their children adore her.

At the death of Baby Clay's father, the ownership of the old man's ring was hotly contested by all the children. But before its fate could be decided, the ring disappeared, and everyone believed that someone had stolen it. They commenced a fruitless search of the house, his belongings, his cars, his office, all the while eyeing one another suspiciously.

Now it is Emma who holds their desire in her hand. She twirls the diamond to catch the light and ponders her situation. A black woman in possession of a rare and expensive ring—found where? In the town dump? Emma knows people who have been punished for much lesser offenses. One of Baby Clay's sisters fired her lifelong servant for putting her bare feet in the swimming pool to cool off on a ninety-eight-degree day when she was living in to babysit the children.

The late-day sun brings the bottle tree to life beside Emma. Blue light dances upward into the sun-bleached branches and downward onto the gray gravel field. She watches the tree in silence, its white limbs graceful bones holding aloft the shimmering blue glass. As Emma watches, she sees what is to come: She sees herself standing before Mr. Clay, producing, from her white satin bodice, the handkerchief, opening the linen square, and holding it out to him. She hears him say, "Jesus Christ, Emma! Where'd you get this?" And her own voice sweetly scolding, "Now, Baby, don't you be takin' the Lord's name in vain."

Then, without a glance of shame, he is no longer her protector in a swamp of discrimination, but a white man named Leslie Clayton Pettit III. No longer Baby Clay, whom she has raised from birth, swiping pureed carrots from his rosy chin with a little silver spoon. He's no longer the child whom she has held down safely on a changing table, blue bunny diaper pins clamped between her teeth while she cooed to make him smile.

Can it be that she is only a servant to him now, a colored woman and, worst of all, a thief? To satisfy the others, will he accuse her? If he does not, he will be the accused. She knows she is expendable in his world.

But Emma McGee is also sanctified, and because she wants to do what is right, she says to herself, "I'll just take it on over there to Baby Clay. He will know what to do."

At five thirty the next morning, Emma arrives in the Pettit kitchen and puts on the coffee. She knows he will be waiting for her to serve it in his study, since everyone else in the household is still sleeping.

"Mornin' Emma," he calls out when she goes in. Her hands tremble slightly as she sets down the tray. She avoids his eyes. "Emma, everything all right?" he asks, quietly now.

"I got something to show you," she says. Licking the corners of her mouth to relieve an unfamiliar drought, she puts her hand into her bodice and withdraws the handkerchief—scorched and wadded.

"What is that?"

"I found it in the dump," she responds and holds it out to him.

"I'm not going to touch that nasty thing, Emma."

She folds back the cloth to reveal the diamond and holds it out again. He picks up the ring with thumb and forefinger and brings it close to his face. His right eye blinks three times, a habit from childhood. A habit she recognizes.

He was six years old when he learned to wink. When he realized he could wink several times in rapid succession, he practiced and practiced till he could do it flawlessly. "Emma, watch me!" he would command, then display his talent, and receive her praise.

"Mmm-mmm-mmm, Baby Clay, ain't you the special one!"

Later, as a teenager, he had to learn not to do this involuntarily, provoking teasing from classmates. Emma is the only one left who knows the truth: It discloses that he has received an unexpected surprise, a powerful secret.

"You go on home now, Emma," he says at last, slipping the ring into his vest pocket.

She stiffens. "Sir?"

His blinking has stopped. But now she is held in thrall by his beloved baby blue eyes.

"Don't 'sir' me, Emma," he says and flashes his best smile.

From a pocket, he pulls out his roll of bills, usually about $1,000 she knows, extracts a $50, and hands it to her, saying, "I told you—go on home now."

searchlights that continuously swept 360 degrees at night. The vast expanse of dreary, regimented, black tar-papered barracks were like the ones we had just left, only this camp looked ten times bigger and I felt one hundred times smaller.

My head whirled as my eyes tried to take in the scene confronting me. A momentary wish flashed through my mind. *This is just a bad dream. I will wake up back home.* It took Mama-san's gentle nudge from behind and her soft voice saying, "Let's go find where we will be staying," to make me realize this was not a nightmare. I stepped down from the train. Just then three young Japanese men walked by, raised their right fists, and yelled, *"Tenno Heika Banzai*—Long live His Majesty the Emperor." People were milling all around us, shouting orders, and flailing their arms as we piled up near the train.

A man in an army truck drove us to our "space," which was 7404 C (block 74, barrack 4, apartment C) in the northwestern corner of the camp. The barracks here were similar to those at Pinedale: 120 feet long, divided into varying sized "apartments," which were nothing more than rectangular rooms with openings above the seven-foot walls. These living spaces extended the full length of the barrack. Any sound made in any one of the living cubicles could be heard throughout the barrack.

When we got to our twenty-feet-by-twenty-feet space, I remarked to my family, "Look, the room is smaller but we don't have to share it with anyone else. That's good." Our parents silently nodded. Looking at the potbellied stove, Yoneichi commented, "Must get cold here." That winter the doorknob would get so cold our fingers would stick to it. We would be plagued by the subfreezing temperatures, scarcely protected by the flimsy barrack walls.

We fell quickly to the task of setting up "home." Papa-san and Yoneichi went to find ticking and straw for our mattresses. Mama-san and I looked around our living space, wondering what we could do to make it ours. There were the familiar army cots and blankets for each of us. Aside from the stove and the light bulb screwed into a ceramic socket on the end of a cord hanging from the ceiling, the room was bare. It was just a space waiting for whatever drama was to be played out here.

My initial shock at seeing the camp for the first time gave way to depression as reality set in. We were going to be here for a while, perhaps forever for all I knew. The drab surroundings and familiar still air of the hot evening crushed whatever small hopes I may have had after leaving Pinedale.

Because of the highly structured way of life in camp there was nothing to do. Many drifted about aimlessly. If they were back at their homes, they would have been working from dawn to dusk at their farms, greenhouses, hotels, restaurants, whatever their business was, in order to make a living. In camp there were many tasks such as garbage collection, fire station watches, and block manager work, but all of these were quickly assigned. Later, the need for adult education classes, arts and crafts, and other creative outlets would become obvious. For now, the overwhelming social problem was simply the monotony. Many people suffered from boredom, bewilderment, and depression.

I longed for the sunny days of spring on Vashon when the fog disappeared in the warmth of the bright sunshine. I imagined the pink and white, fragrant carnations along the sides of our farmhouse. I thought about the quiet evenings, so still I could hear an ambitious woodpecker hammering into a distant tree. I especially missed our green lawn where I could lie down after a day's work and watch fluffy, white clouds, resembling horses, flowers, buildings, or a palace, float across the blue sky.

Far from the greenness of Vashon, Tule Lake internment camp was plagued with unpredictable dust storms that came and went as if the desert were throwing a furious tantrum. They would leave us gasping for breath as we ran for shelter. Covering our faces with handkerchiefs or some clothing was essential. The slightest breeze would pick up the dirt and swirl it around the barracks, chasing us as we scrambled for cover.

After we had been in Tule Lake for a few weeks, I learned that my dance instructor, Mrs. Nakamura, had been asked to present a program at an upcoming event. She was well known in Seattle as an instructor and player of the *shamisen,* a Japanese stringed instrument. These programs were the first attempts to relieve the monotony of internment by using the talents of the community. Mama-san was pleased that Ardith and I were selected to perform, and so was I. It was a great honor, but I wasn't sure about dancing in front of a large and unfamiliar audience.

Ardith and I practiced together diligently. We followed Mrs. Nakamura's instructions precisely as she strummed on the shamisen. Listening and dancing to the rhythm of the music, I escaped from the dreariness and fear of the camp. I was carried back to our teacher's spacious living room on Vashon where Ardith and I had practiced together. The room provided an atmosphere of beauty and serenity.

As we danced to the music traditionally played in a minor key, I had a vision of a pensive person walking beside a gentle stream trickling over rocks. The water followed the bends in the river, finally flowing into a serene pool. The music and the movements took me to a peaceful place where the two cultures unified for a brief time. I felt whole—Japanese by heritage and American by birth.

Ardith and I moved our bodies slowly and gracefully, making each step with the bend of the knees. Each head, arm, and hand movement, each turn of the body flowed together into the next position. We practiced until Mrs. Nakamura felt confident in our movements.

The evening of our performance finally arrived. Several ladies helped us put on our beautiful kimonos that Mrs. Nakamura borrowed from some families at the camp. Ardith's had red, purple, and gold leaves on a beige background with a red obi interwoven with silver threads. Mine was a dark blue kimono with soft, simple patterns in gray. My obi was also red with silver threads.

Getting dressed in kimonos is a lengthy, complicated process. I was prepared to stand for quite awhile as the ladies helped me into each successive garment. As they tugged and pulled the sashes snugly around me, I noticed beads of perspiration on their foreheads and upper lips.

First came the short-sleeved undershirt tied at the waist, followed by the under robe, which is long and visible only at the neck like the collar of a shirt. Next we put on the kimono, which is heavy and long. It must be folded up and tied with a cord to hold it in place. This was followed by a wide long obi, which the women wound tightly around my waist several times making it impossible to take a deep breath or take long bold steps. Then they tied the obi into a special knot on my back and held it in place with various cords and clasps. With white *tabi*—Japanese socks—and *geta*—wooden clogs on our feet, and red lipstick, we were ready. Mama-san gave me her last-minute advice, "This is an opportunity to represent the Vashon Japanese community—so do your very best."

We arrived at the outdoor platform where a crowd had gathered to watch our performance. It felt almost unbearably hot in my heavy kimono in the still air of the darkening desert skies. Mrs. Nakamura, dressed in her muted colored kimono, stepped onto the stage and seated herself on a chair. Holding her shamisen on her lap, she smiled and nodded at us confidently.

As I approached the platform, my stomach fluttered, but I was full of energy as if I had shrugged off the oppression of the environment. Ardith and I took our positions in the center of the stage and waited to begin our dance. In that moment, I knew we brought hope to the audience, representing the beauty and value of our culture.

Suddenly, the revolving searchlight from a nearby watchtower flashed across my face, blinding me momentarily. I dropped my eyes and froze. My legs felt heavy, my arms like stone. I struggled to regain my composure. Vulnerability and fragility exposed my old confusion: *Am I Japanese or am I American in this barbed-wire camp, about to perform a Japanese dance?* I was chilled to the bone in the hot desert air and sick to my stomach. *Can I really do this?*

As I waited for the cue to begin, I told myself, *Listen for the first stroke on the shamisen. Concentrate on each step. Remember what Mama-san said.* I glanced out over the crowd toward Mama-san. She looked at me, smiled, and nodded her head.

On the third strum of the music, I slowly turned my head to the right and raised my right hand higher than my left in front of my body. My hands opened like the wings of a crane. Bending my knees, I slid my right foot slightly ahead of my left. *Forget everything else and move with the music,* I told myself. *I know the steps by heart.* As if suspended in time and space, I numbly and automatically made each movement, step by step. Gradually the movements of my body and the rhythm and tone of the shamisen took over until I realized that Ardith and I *were* dancing, and dancing well together. Relief, self-confidence, and even some self-importance finally crept back in as I gained a sense of the appreciative audience. *Now enjoy the dance.* And I did. I had finally found my own place in this barren camp.

We had only been dancing a couple of minutes when, suddenly, a blast of hot wind whipped up the fine dust, swirling it everywhere between the barracks and across the open spaces, especially at us on the exposed, elevated platform. It felt like a thousand bees were stinging my hands and face.

Mrs. Nakamura stopped playing. We covered our noses and mouths and scrambled off the platform in our beautiful kimonos. Everyone scattered like leaves before a giant blower. Ardith and I took cover behind the closest barrack. By then Ardith's hair, kimono, and obi were coated with fine dust. It clung to the bangs on her forehead, to her eyelids and eyelashes, and stuck to her lipstick. Tears ran down her dusty cheeks. When she brushed the tears aside, the dust left a smudge across her cheek. I must have looked like a dust ball myself. Then the storm died down as abruptly as it had started.

When I got home, dust had penetrated through the cracks in the loose-fitting window, under the door, and up through the floorboards. Like thick smoke that streamed out of a smoldering fire, it seeped through everything in its path, filling every nook and cranny. It seemed as if God was speaking through the dust storm, creating in me a crisis of identity. It was as though God Himself was saying, "No." I wasn't accepted in the white community, but when I tried to be Japanese, I felt annihilated. I threw myself on my cot and sobbed. Mama-san sat down beside me, lifted me into her arms, and silently rocked me back and forth until my crying subsided.

That was the last time Ardith and I danced together. Before the year was over, we would be separated forever. My family would be sent to the Heart Mountain Relocation Center in Wyoming and Ardith's family would go to the Topaz Relocation Center in Utah. Ardith's ultimate goal was to travel to the East Coast to be with Hanako, her older sister. Our letters flew back and forth for months. Then they stopped.

Months after our dance in the dust storm, a letter came from Hanako telling me that Ardith had died from an unknown disease. When I read that, I rushed outdoors, stumbling and looking at the barbed-wire fence in the foreground. I raised my clenched fists into the air and shouted "Ardith" in anguish. A strong wind swooped down, picking up the fine dirt and sent it surging through the air, blinding me. I took cover behind the closest barrack and crumpled to the ground, sobbing.

I pictured Ardith's large, beautiful eyes, her black shiny hair against her clear, creamy skin. *How beautiful and graceful she looked as she danced with me on the stage*, I thought. *I will never see her again.* Our dance in the searchlight was Ardith's last, and in that moment I decided it would be my last dance, too.

Excerpted from Mary Matsuda Gruenewald's book, *Looking Like the Enemy: My Story of Imprisonment in Japanese-American Internment Camps*, Copyright © 2005 by NewSage Press. Reprinted by permission of NewSage Press. www. newsagepress.com

FIRST TO LET GO

By: Elizabeth Van Deventer

I wedged my aching body up in a shea tree as the huge West African sun sank quickly below the horizon. Hands trembling in the fading light, I reached into my goatskin sack and pulled out a devastating letter my mother had just sent from Virginia. I looked again at the photo she'd included of my eldest brother Jack.

He stood among tropical plants in the San Francisco Arboretum, a baseball cap covering his bald head, a potbelly protruding from emaciated limbs, his eyes sunken in, his face gaunt. Gone was his thick, wavy, dark blond hair, his fit, muscular physique, his tan, the glow in his eyes.

As I bit my parched lips, my red, swollen eyes followed my mother's words numbly yet again across two pages of yellow, lined notepad paper with a fading hope that somehow I'd misunderstood.

"I'm so sorry to have to send this to you, Betsy. I don't know what to do but just tell it to you like it is. Jack is dying of AIDS . . ."

"No!" I shouted, my voice echoing off cliffs in the distance.

Once, when I was twelve, I hid behind a chair watching my mother weeping as she and my father clutched a scribbled note from Jack saying he'd run away from home. He was sixteen. He'd bought a one-way ticket to San Francisco when he realized he couldn't be gay in rural Virginia. They were devastated; all they'd ever wanted was for him to be happy.

Now, at twenty-five, I was fulfilling my dream to be a Peace Corps volunteer in Africa. Yet as the hot Sahel breeze blew tears across my cheeks, I knew I needed to go home. Quickly, I stuffed the letter back inside the sack as black clouds filled the sky and torrents of rain soaked me to the skin.

"How could you do this to my brother!" I shrieked, flailing my arms into the storm.

In Mali, where death is a big part of life, crying openly is frowned upon. So I'd ridden my motorcycle far into the bush to mourn alone. Now, covered in bee stings, after two days of sleeping in trees and being wedged inside snake-filled rock cliffs, I returned to my village to say good-bye.

"You're leaving us?" the village chief asked sadly, holding my hand lightly in a gesture of friendship. As I fought off tears, women dressed in colorful headscarves and skirts clucked disapprovingly. "No, no. You must not cry," they scolded. To them, crying was for funerals, where *griots,* the storytellers of Africa, would sing mournfully for the whole village.

Two weeks later, in October 1990, I stepped off an Amtrak train in San Francisco. As my taxi sped through the streets, my palms grew clammy and my head spun. I didn't know how I could help Jack when I was such a mess myself. I just knew I had to do it.

Finally, I stood in a narrow hallway outside his apartment struggling to adjust to such an abrupt shift in my life. I leaned my aching head against the wall, still hearing the rhythmic thud of wooden mortars pounding millet in pestles across the village, smelling the aroma of smoky river fish cooking in shea oil, and feeling the soft dirt floor of mud huts on my bare feet. Even now, as I braced myself to knock on Jack's door, a part of me was still in Africa.

I pulled my shoulders back, trying for the first time in my life to be the strong one to an older brother who'd always been in charge. I took a deep breath and knocked. There was a quick rumbling of feet; then the door flung open dramatically.

"She's here! She's here," my brother cried.

I'd practiced my smile and held it now as if it were hair sprayed on my face. Jack's small, thin body danced around excitedly, his bony legs dangling under loose, Fruit of the Loom, white, cotton briefs. His thin stubble of hair stood on end, his gray skin fragile like a hornet's nest. Beneath dark circles and bloated cheeks, his beautiful smile looked like it had been transplanted on a dying body.

"Ohhhh," he sighed, reaching out to hug me, then stopped. "Wait a minute," he choked, putting his hand to his mouth. "I've got to throw up." He scurried into the bathroom, slamming the door behind him. Staring blankly into his tiny efficiency apartment, I suddenly felt the air sucked out of me.

Across the immaculate room, his Siamese cat, Sesame, lay curled up in a ball on a small tan futon as if the loud retching sounds from the bathroom were something she'd long grown used to. My eyes scanned my brother's belongings: his camera equipment on a white art table, a shelf with books on Ansel Adams and John Muir, Mexican wall hangings from his travels, kitschy figurines here and there.

Jack was only thirty. He'd just finished a landscape photography degree at the San Francisco Art Institute. He was an outdoorsy, vegetarian health nut. *He can't just die!* I thought.

Suddenly, Jack flung open the bathroom door and then bounced down onto his bed across from me, laughing as if nothing odd were happening.

"Dr. Katz says I'm going to die in two weeks."

"Two weeks! What does he know?" I gasped, unable to grasp that my brother would die at all. "You're *not* going to die in two weeks!" I said, outraged. "Dr. Katz doesn't know what he's talking about."

Jack sat quietly on the bed, a look of clarity coming over his face. "You're right. I'm not going to listen to him!" He stood up confidently, arms tight at his sides.

When I saw his whole demeanor brighten, a part of me was scared that I'd given him false hope; while another part of me recognized it as the one thing we both needed to survive.

He waltzed into the small kitchen space, his knees like large knuckles on sticks, and began punching numbers on a cordless phone. "I've *just got* to call Michael Rose. She's having a Halloween party tomorrow night." Michael was one of Jack's oldest friends.

"Oh Taffy, you'll never in a million years guess what?" he said into the phone, hand on his bony protruding hip. "My sister's here from Africa and she says I'm *not* going to die in two weeks!" He stood up pin straight. "So I'm coming to your Halloween party after all!" Then he held out the phone as squeals of deep, joyous laughter spewed out like a tonic for our pain.

Halloween night, Jack and I sat next to each other in a large, plush red velour chair. Jack wore a checkered cap, crisp white tuxedo shirt, and a black bow tie. We watched Michael brace himself against his dining-room table as a crew of men in sparkly dresses and pumps adjusted the hooks of his falsies. Suddenly, I felt dowdy in my blue print African shirt and khaki pants.

"Time for your wig now, Taffy!" Jack winked playfully.

"Oh, the trouble we girls go through to look beautiful!" Michael fawned, batting his false eyelashes. I couldn't imagine that four years later, Michael would fly to Virginia for my wedding, his emaciated AIDS-wracked body dragging an oxygen tank down the aisle.

"This way," Jack said, as we scurried through the streets after Michael's three-foot-tall, white wig that rose above the costumed crowd like a lighthouse beacon. In black leather chaps, vests, and caps, groups of men swayed erotically to the throbbing electronic bass blaring out of open bars as drag queens gave mock kisses with their engorged lips at gawking passersby.

For a moment, I drifted back to a funeral in Mali, hearing griots pluck strings on handmade koras and tap wooden xylophones with sticks. I could see men dressed as antelope circling the deceased, while bare-breasted women rapidly shifted their hips to the ancient rhythms.

For some time after Halloween, Jack and I lived off the false high of that party. Dr. Katz's two weeks came and went, and Jack started to seem better. His T-cell count went up, and his life expectancy was increased to three months. I began to assume he'd never die.

Every night, I fell asleep as Jack heaved in the bathroom. Like Sesame, I became used to it all so quickly. Every morning, Jack would stand in his underwear at the kitchen counter popping a handful of pills from a neatly organized plastic, compartmentalized box. Then he'd look out the window. "What are we going to do today?" he'd ask himself with a twinge of hope.

On days when Jack felt too sick to go out, he'd sit with Sesame, sipping peppermint tea amidst the smell of incense and the ethereal music of the Cocteau Twins. He'd spend hours making shadow boxes with intricate scenes, each one telling a story about what it was like to die of AIDS. I'd sit on a stool at the kitchen window, writing memories of Africa in my journal, unaware that AIDS was silently spreading there, too.

When Jack was feeling good, he'd have friends over or want to go for a drive. One day, driving us to Golden Gate Park, he suddenly swerved across busy lanes of traffic, heading right into oncoming cars. As we both screamed, I grabbed the wheel and pulled us back.

"Oh, God, this brain tumor is starting to make me crazy," he wept into his pillow that night, his pain like a corkscrew spiraling through my heart.

"It's okay, honey, we can't afford to pay the parking anyway," I lied later when I sold his car. Really, I couldn't bear to tell him he'd never drive again.

After a month, my Peace Corps stipend began to dwindle and Jack's unpaid bills piled up. My parents had already sent us a lot of money, and I couldn't bear to ask them for more. Unable to see how little time we had left, I searched for a job.

"My brother has AIDS and I need to pay the bills," I said too honestly, my hands shaking as I filled out application after application. I never heard back. Finally, someone in the AIDS network got me a job at a shampoo company.

"This is Elizabeth from Tri shampoo," I'd say in a fake perky voice to salons across the city as I sat in the overly perfumed office, feeling as fragile as a crumpled leaf. "May I take your order?"

As time went on, I began crying in the shower to keep up my strong appearance. "I can hear you crying in there," Jack said anxiously through the bathroom door. I stood frozen, suddenly quiet, caught red-handed as water washed away my tears.

I didn't want Jack to know what a wreck I was, so I walked thirteen blocks up to Buena Vista Park looking for a place to cry. I scouted behind trees and shrubs, pretending I was analyzing the flora and fauna only to stumble across people fornicating behind bushes, making out in the grass, or sleeping drunk under benches.

"Ugh, I can't even find a place to cry," I mumbled sadly, then laughed at the absurdity. Here I was in the middle of this city trying to find a hidden place to grieve, just like in Mali.

One night in December, Jack was feeling so good we decided to go to a bar. As we walked in, a man sneered, "Hey, no sick faggots in here." Jack kept walking as my heart sank.

"Oh Betsy," he sighed. "Some people can be so mean." He aimed his camera at the bar mirror and took a photo of us in the reflection. "You just have to go on and have a good time anyway."

Then one sunny day in late January, Jack and I sat on a patch of grass in Golden Gate Park. Jack lit a cigarette and took a drag. Then he smiled in a settled way. "I know I'm going to die," he said calmly.

I stared at smoke rising upward from his lips as a childhood memory came to me with new meaning. "I remember one time when we were bareback on the horses at the edge of a large, open pasture," I began.

Jack looked at me wide-eyed.

"Red and Socks were tugging on their reins to be let free. I was so nervous trying to hold back Socks, but you just smiled and let go of Red's reins. Then he bolted forward!" I said, shooting my arm out over my legs. "And Socks lunged after him. They galloped like mad, snorting, hooves pounding. I clung to a handful of Socks' black mane, terrified of falling." Jack leaned toward me, the ember of his cigarette growing large.

"I heard you laughing like crazy ahead of me and you know what?" He shook his head. "You helped me forget my fear so I could just enjoy the ride," I said excitedly, remembering the freeing feeling. I looked down at the grass, searching for a way to explain what all this meant for us now.

"We're all going to die. You're just bravely letting go of the reins first, just like you did back then," I said. "You were always first at things."

Jack took a long drag.

"I love you, Betsy. Here, have a cigarette," he said, passing me his pack of American Spirits. "Lord knows you could use one."

A few days later, I marched in panic into the hospice where Jack's visiting nurse had taken him while I was at work. Clearly, she had known that Jack wouldn't live much longer. Soon, making visits to the hospice became my new routine. It was too hard for me to accept that this was the end.

Then, one afternoon, as I sat taking shampoo orders, my mom called from the hospice where she'd been with Jack soon after he'd arrived.

"They say he's not gonna make it through the night," she said, weeping.

"What?" I cried in disbelief, feeling it all happening too fast. "But I've got a job, and I thought we'd make it all work out somehow," I mumbled as she hung up the phone.

When I saw Jack lying in his bed, his eyes rolling open and closed, his chest limply rising and falling, I stared at him, now obviously dying, suddenly aware of my deep denial. My mother, my brother David, and Jack's friends all gathered around his bed, holding his hands, patting his legs, wiping their eyes, their lips quivering as they talked softly to him.

"Oh, Johnny," Michael Rose sobbed, struggling to contain tears for his friend, not knowing his fate would one day mirror Jack's.

My father and brother Matt, who couldn't get flights in time, told Jack they loved him through the phone. Shortly after, his eyes rolled back into his head, and a small sound echoed from his body as he took his last breath. And then he was gone.

As my Mom hugged Jack's body, her deep pain unbearable to even acknowledge, a nurse tapped my shoulder. "The man from the crematorium is here," she whispered, gesturing down the hall. My eyes went wide in shock as I turned to look at my mom, not wanting her to have to deal with such a harsh job so soon, not ready for it myself.

Abruptly, I was sitting across from a thin, pale, balding man in a gray suit with a tight smile. He checked off squares as I answered his questions robotically: address, phone number, payment plan, style of container, ashes in large or small chunks? My mind wandered back to Mali, the whole village dancing ceremoniously around the deceased wrapped lovingly in handwoven cloth, the shaking of cowry shells. I could hear the mournful braying of African donkeys at dawn, like griots wailing the collective grief of the ancestors.

Then I found myself standing with Mom like a statue on a darkly lit street corner. The cold February wind blew as we waited for a train. Brakes squealed to a stop. Every part of my body felt battered and bruised as we stepped into bright glaring lights, past a blur of people, to hard plastic seats.

The train rolled on. Slowly sounds filtered through my numbness: muffled music buzzing under headphones, newspapers flashing open and closed, mumbled whispers, people clearing their throats.

I looked up. No one on this train had any idea that my brother had just died, that my mother was crushed with grief, that my whole life had fallen apart. It was just a normal day for these people. I wanted to shout at them angrily. How dare they keep going on with their lives!

In that moment, the last four months folded together like an accordion in my mind: Malian women in colorful garb clucking disapprovingly as I cried in the park, Michael Rose's raucous laughter blurring into my sobs, Jack snapping our photo at the bar as he took his last breath.

Suddenly, the reality of his death hit me like a hurled stone, the immensity of pain shattering every nerve. I sat there, empty.

Then I glanced around again at the other passengers. An old man clutched his bags nervously, a weary look in his eyes. A scrawny teenage boy sat slumped over, his head resting on a stack of books. A young woman in a business suit leaned against the pole in the aisle next to me, her eyes closed. I could see myself mirrored in them. They too had suffered in ways I did not know. We were all like Malians—walking around hiding our pain, our grief, our stories.

A flush of warmth filled me: *Imagine if we treated everyone as if they'd suffered like us.*

THE HORN OF AFRICA

By: Suzanne Montagne

Like a flock of migratory birds, the African women swoop down on the labor and delivery unit of a Seattle hospital, their swirling veils contrasting with their long, windswept skirts. It is sometimes impossible to tell which one is pregnant, wrapped as they are in layers of cloth. Assembled at the nurse's station, they stand still and wait. The pregnant one stands in the center of the group, silent.

Their scent hangs on the air, spicy and warm, as if they have been cooking together. One woman's long tapered hand is covered with a filigree of black henna tattoos. When I ask her about this, she blushes and tells me that she is a new bride. If I could see her feet, I know that they, too, would be decorated with flowers and vines.

As a nurse, I am fortunate to be privy to this veiled, secret world and feel connected to women who come together to bring the next baby into the world. They seem to feel a bond with me, too, and we are at ease with each other, in spite of the language difference.

"Will she have to have the monitors put on her?" one woman who speaks English asks. She is holding a sheer, coffee brown veil in front of her. Embellished with clusters of gold threaded flowers, the veil lights up her beautiful dark brown complexion.

"Yes," I tell them. "I want to listen to the baby's heartbeat for about twenty minutes. If everything sounds good, we can take the monitors off so she can move around and walk."

In their nomadic culture, childbirth is a dangerous rite of passage. In sub-Saharan Africa, one in forty-eight women dies in childbirth from hemorrhage, infection, or prolonged/obstructed labor.

Nursing and midwifery transcend social boundaries, allowing for immediate intimacy. These women trust my touch—trust that I will keep them safe. For them, birthing is a private world, a space that men rarely violate.

These African women care for each other deeply; it is very unusual for them to labor or deliver alone. Children are the precious continuation of the ancestral line.

A laboring mother of ten children once told me with a wide smile, "Twenty-five members of my family were killed in my country, and I am replacing them one by one."

In the labor room, there is a flurry of activity. Chairs are lined up and the eldest sits down, watching me with a regal and curious expression. They want to know how we handle this most important event in a woman's life.

The younger women stand behind their elders around the labor bed. The older women who speak English answer my questions. Giggling quietly to each other, the teenagers exhibit an American body language while dressed in the long traditional skirts and veils of Africa. Slouching against the wall, their headscarves fall back onto their shoulders, revealing gold hoop earrings and plastic barrettes.

They are part of a matriarchal line, initiates into a sacred circle. This female community embraces and supports these young women as they gain power within their families through birthing and mothering.

The pregnant woman says, "My name is Omal," and smiles. The other women look on approvingly. Her smooth brown face glows with pleasure. We are gathered to attend the birth of her baby, and her pride outweighs her shyness.

Smaller and more compact than many of the other women, Omal kicks off her sandals, exposing the broad feet of a barefoot childhood. I place monitors on her belly. Careful not to expose her unnecessarily, I reach under her hospital gown to feel her baby, which kicks at my hands from within its firm round melon. We laugh as the baby reaches its feet and hands toward the warm areas my touch creates on Omal's body.

With the strong rhythmic beat of the baby's heart on the fetal monitor as background music, we sit and talk. I want Omal and the other women to feel comfortable with me before the next step of my labor assessment—the cervical exam. Uncomfortable but routine for most pregnant women, it will be both physically and emotionally difficult because Omal is undoubtedly circumcised, and very likely infibulated, which means that her clitoris and labia have been removed and the edges sewn together, leaving only an opening the size of a pencil top.

When Somalis first immigrated to the United States, there was shock and confusion amongst the nurses and doctors who cared for them during their pregnancies. They would not talk freely to us through the male interpreters that we had, so one female physician trained female interpreters, and a dialogue with these women began.

Gathered in the nurse's station, we asked this doctor the questions we could not ask our patients during their labors: Why the genital removal? How and when is the birth canal opened for delivery? How do we care for these scarred perineums before and after birth? Together, we learned what these women wanted and needed during their deliveries.

Two of our nurses were from Eritrea and Nigeria, and although they were reluctant to discuss the details of how deliveries are handled in their country, they defended the practice as a cultural (not religious) norm. They said that we as Americans had no right to challenge the rituals of another culture. It was the first step in reaching across a great divide and becoming more educated and open to each other.

Since the time of the pharaohs, female circumcision has been part of their culture. As religions focused on dominance over nature, men took ownership of the birth canal, believing evil entered women's bodies through the vagina. Women could not be trusted to control their sexual urges. The worth of a woman is based on this "purity" and so uncircumcised women are ostracized. It is a cruel twist that the fierce bonding between these women comes at the cost of perpetuating this dark ritual.

Girls are circumcised between the ages of four and nine. The women in their family hold them down and check to be sure the entire clitoris has been removed and the vaginal opening is small enough. They share a culture of pain. The tiny opening causes a backup of urine and menstrual blood. Urinary tract infections as well as chronic pelvic and back pain are common.

On a bride's wedding night, her husband, or one of his aunts, may use a small knife to cut the scarred vaginal opening wider. It is very important to keep this opening minimal, as it is believed this keeps women safe from sexual advances and their own desires. Full penetration may not be achieved. Consummating a marriage may take weeks, or hours, depending on the patience of a woman's husband. Conception through this narrow passage may also be difficult.

By the time a woman is ready for her first delivery, the vaginal opening has been somewhat stretched and enlarged, but many women die or suffer injuries during childbirth because of their circumcisions. They cannot control their labors as uncut women in other cultures do.

Babies are delivered after deep cuts or tears are made below the vagina, sometimes extending all the way to the rectum. Women often develop fistulas—openings between the vaginal and rectal or bladder walls, after tearing. Despite these complications, it is the pubic hood, the flap of skin closed over the front of the genitals and the tiny opening that they feel is important to maintain.

Some Somali women tell us their husbands do not like the circumcisions and the pain they cause their wives. Now that they are living in a culture that allows them the choice, many do not plan to circumcise their daughters. During meetings between our physician and these women, an agreement was reached. This physician would lightly nick their infant daughters' clitoral hoods as a symbolic gesture to the ancient cultural ritual of their ancestors.

Grandmothers are honored in this culture, and so my age and silver hair help Omal's family to trust me. I am older than most of them, and they wait for me to direct the conversation.

"Is this your first baby?" I ask.

Omal smiles and looks over at a tall woman with a bright green veil, who answers for her.

"She has a son and a daughter already."

"Are you her sister?" I ask.

"I am her oldest sister," she tells me with pride. "And these are our other sisters." She waves her hand, and a dozen slim gold bracelets slide down her walnut brown arm.

"How many sisters altogether?" I ask, thinking of my own four sisters and how we shared one bedroom as children.

"There are twelve girls in our family. Two are still in Somalia," she says. "Our father's other wives had boys."

She tells me about growing up in their father's cluster of small houses, one for each of his five wives. Their mother was the first wife, which gave them a higher status.

"The wives have completely separate households and do not visit each other, but it is very fun for the kids," she explains, "because it is a village of sisters and brothers. We play and take care of each other."

All are involved in discussing Omal's birth plan. Decisions about anesthesia, baths, walking during labor, and breastfeeding are collective. Omal waits for a consensus before making decisions.

I finally ask Omal if I can check her cervix, and she reluctantly agrees. Several women leave. Only two sisters remain. There is a tense silence. They watch my face. I have trained myself to not react to the flat, vacant pubic area. Inside, I recoil as if I can feel the raw pain of this wound in my own body. Omal's perineum is a wall of scars.

Usually, two fingers are used to feel the edges of the cervix, but with Omal, only one finger will fit. It is strange territory inside of her vagina.

I feel what might be cervix, a bag of amniotic fluid, or the baby's head. Omal tenses and I can feel her tiny vaginal opening clench shut. It is difficult to know if this reaction is physical pain or the emotional pain of feeling exposed.

Omal's cervix feels thick and closed. There is no blood on my glove, so it is probably not yet thinning or opening. She relaxes once I am finished, and I help her to pull the blankets up to her chin. The two sisters leave to find the other women, so I am alone with Omal.

She has already been opened and closed twice for her other deliveries, so it is doubtful that there will be much stretch around her vaginal opening. "Do you want to be sewn up as small as you are now after you deliver?" I ask gingerly.

She pauses. I can tell that she is considering her options, knowing that she will be considered less desirable if she does not conform to tradition. If her older sisters were in the room, they would have answered that she wanted to be sewn up to the same size again.

"I would like to have the opening to be bigger," she answers, and then adds in a whisper, "My daughter is not circumcised." And I understand that this is her secret from the others.

"I'll let your midwife know, so that you don't need to discuss it in front of anyone later on," I tell her.

Omal spends the next several hours pacing around her room. Her husband comes to visit, holding their five-year-old son by the hand and carrying their two-year-old daughter on his hip. He is joyous, with a wide-open smile. This is a culture that cherishes their children. The young boy stands beside his father, holding fast to his side. He stares at all of these familiar women sitting next to his mother's bed.

The little girl smiles and waves at her mother and aunts. Clearly, this group of women makes her feel safe in spite of the hospital environment. Omal's older sister takes her niece onto her lap and one of the teenage girls reties her many corkscrew braids. Her father leaves her with her aunt, and takes his son out to the waiting room, which is now full of uncles, grandfathers, and male cousins. They will wait all night, until the baby is born.

As Omal's labor progresses, I walk with her and feel the rigidity of her back. She is holding this baby in, away from her scarred birth canal. As her baby moves lower in her body, Omal holds her legs together, rigid and straight, as if this could stop the natural flow of life. Eventually, she climbs into her bed and moans with her contractions.

The teenagers look startled. Omal's daughter is singing and laying her cheek against the small breast of one of the girls. Anxious to go, she carries Omal's little girl and leaves the room. Soon, the other women drift toward the waiting room.

I put my hand in Omal's.

She looks at me and moans. She is in transition, that part of labor when the cervix is stretched and pulled open by the pressure of the descending head of the baby. It's a very intense stage: Even the calmest women tend to lose their focus and panic.

Women shake uncontrollably during transition. Birth requires the mother to open her body up wide and push an actual part of herself out from the center of her being. It can feel like dying.

Women who have experienced sexual trauma, be it a traditional ritual, like circumcision, or an assault, often try to detach themselves from their bodies. Whatever damaging experience they have had, it often returns during labor on a very deep, visceral level. I have seen real terror in their faces when the baby comes into the birth canal, and the damaged tissue of their bodies begins to stretch and thin.

Sitting against her bank of pillows, Omal rolls her head from side to side, afraid and closed off from us. Placing my hands on her warm face, I stare into her eyes.

"Omal . . . ," I say. "Look at me."

She looks away.

"Omal . . . ," I call again. Using two fingers, I point at my eyes. "Keep looking at me. Stay focused."

She looks back at me, worried.

The midwife's calm voice encourages Omal. "You're ready to push. I'm going to sit here and hold your bottom. I won't let you tear. Go ahead and push."

She has made a cut below Omal's tiny vaginal opening. The thick scar tissue barely bleeds. Omal's legs are propped against the bed. She stares back. The smell rising off of her skin is acidic and electric. Instead of pushing down, Omal gasps and pulls the corners of her mouth down, like a mask, and squeezes her eyes shut. I realize she is reliving the day she was cut.

The scent of saltwater is released as the amniotic sac breaks. In the whiteness of the hospital linens, Omal's dark brown skin is like a bank of rich earth. The trickle of fluid pools like spring water in the bed. The baby's heart beats a rapid rhythm from the monitor.

As Omal pushes, her vagina bulges outward. The baby is coming fast. We see a small circle of slick black hair, first the size of a quarter, then bigger. Omal focuses and then grabs her knees in a deep squat on the bed.

The smooth, dark wall between her legs starts to open up, showing deep red edges around a glistening, wet head. The baby emerges from the scarred surface of Omal's body and rotates around. The face is reddened from exertion, and the long almond eyes look surprised.

A fat, round baby slides out of Omal and into the midwife's hands, who stands up immediately and puts the new baby directly on Omal's skin, between her breasts. Omal's vaginal opening is almost a normal size now, and the swollen edges resemble her lost labia. Although these women have tried to sew the door to the womb closed, life keeps coming through it.

The baby can smell her mother and starts to root around for the breast. This new child is a girl, and we all laugh and congratulate Omal. I wrap mother and child with layers of warmed soft blankets.

Omal gazes, lovestruck, into her baby's little face. She doesn't seem to notice as a local anesthetic is injected into her swollen vagina. Carefully the midwife sews the raw edges together again with a larger opening.

The instruments and placenta are removed from the room, and soon the whole family will come in to celebrate, bringing food from home and oatmeal soup for Omal to sip. I gently take Omal's breast in my hand and place it in her baby's mouth. The baby suckles and blissfully closes her lovely dark eyes. Her little body relaxes, her hands resting against the sides of Omal's breast, and her round brown legs, slightly open, reveal a perfect rosebud.

RISK

Once we believe in ourselves, we can risk curiosity, wonder, spontaneous delight, or any experience that reveals the human spirit.

e. e. cummings

RUMOUR OF RED

By: Marlene Blessing

Mrs. Parlato's lips bloomed with deep color like a sweet red rose in spring. Her long, dark hair was thick and glossy, held in a plump braid that hugged the nape of her neck. Often, she wore a bright blue, felt Mexican jacket, appliqued with palm trees, men napping beneath sombreros, donkeys being led to market, and prickly cacti. When she spoke, her rich voice delivered promises and yeses sweet as a candy dish full of caramels.

I was mesmerized by my second-grade teacher. She seemed like a beautiful heroine in a fairy tale, someone who could pull out a wand and *crunch, crackle* make thorny branches part and snap to reveal a glowing secret passage that would help me escape impending boredom. Such was her power on my imagination. I wanted to follow her everywhere.

Each day in class, she brought a story and artifacts to transport my classmates and me to foreign lands. After the monotony of reciting multiplication tables and practicing cursive writing (I especially loved the lowercase q for being a backward g), we would leap with our teacher to a place on the globe, transfixed as she described plants and animals and foods and every comfort and discomfort we might find within such a land.

To further sweeten my days of learning, Mrs. Parlato gave me a special assignment to write and perform small puppet plays for the class each week. I learned to guide the marionette's strings so it could sweep its arms wide, shake its legs and torso excitedly, and clack its red wooden lips in time with my dialogue. It was my chance to take Mrs. Parlato and the whole class to new imaginary places. I felt elevated to the status of storyteller. Just like her.

One rainy, blustery Seattle day, as we sat in our flimsy 1950s portable building with raindrops pelting the roof, she taught us to sing "My Little Grass Shack in Kealakekua, Hawaii." No child was left behind as she encouraged us to repeat and repeat the exciting new name of the song's fish— *humuhumunukunukuapua'a*. It was a happy mouthful for each of us, sugary vowel after vowel slipsliding on our tongues.

Hula lessons followed, with my boyfriend, Petey Robinson, shaking it with me as we swayed next to our bolted-down desks. We were up and out of our seats, grooving to our favorite new song, lifting our little round noses into the air to imagine a whiff of salty sea breezes. School was a mere three blocks from Alki Beach and Puget Sound, so we didn't have to struggle to conjure that scent. The only dance Mrs. Parlato taught us that rivaled that sensual island hula was a Spanish flamenco. Loaded with black wooden castanets, all thirty-eight of us clicked and clacked them with our hands and stomped our feet furiously to show how devotedly Spanish we could all be. *Olé, Olé!* we hollered.

I could never shake off my bad habit of "disturbing" my neighbors—that was always included in her comments on my report cards—but I knew I was still teacher's pet, her favorite, the crème de la crème of Mrs. Parlato's class. Being absent from school was unimaginable for me. It would mean missing an adventure with Mrs. Parlato. It would mean not being able to scoop up new words and customs and visions from faraway places. I couldn't miss being carried away.

One morning, just before the entire class was about to explode out the doors for early recess on the cement playground, Mrs. Parlato crooked her finger and gestured for me to step to her desk. Then she dismissed everyone else to play four-square or tetherball, hang from the monkey bars, or spin wildly on the horizontal steel bars. I was relieved that I wouldn't have to be chased once again by chubby little Davie Carlson, whose crush on me was so naked and doomed. He seemed always to have a runny nose with dirt smeared in it. I had watched him wipe snot on his plaid flannel sleeves more than once. He was my Caliban, a clumsy suitor who would never succeed. No, today I would have special time with Mrs. Parlato, a private conversation that might reveal some new surprise.

"Today," she began slowly, "you will move to a desk on the other side of the portable. You finish your lessons so quickly and well that we want you to move up to the third grade. That's where you will be from now on. How does that sound?" I felt tiny ripples of electricity zigzagging throughout my body. Third grade? Third grade! Could it be true that I would slide right into a desk with the big kids? That I would be one of them? Instantly?

Ours was a split classroom, a common phenomenon in post-World War II schools as a tsunami of baby boomers flooded pre-war facilities. Makeshift prefab portable buildings were plunked side by side like tiny wooden houses on a Monopoly board to hold the overflow. Poorly insulated buildings, they barely contained the clattering curiosity of elementary school children. Because two grade levels of students had been spliced together in our portable, snippets of knowledge from the advanced assignments of the third graders flowed to the edges of the second graders' rows of wooden desks. By listening closely, eavesdropping really, I learned that the third graders were studying something called "fractions," bits of numbers like wedges of a pie.

Now, only months into the school year, I would be one of them. Mrs. Parlato had chosen me. I could check out more advanced books from the school library. *Wizard of Oz, By the Shores of Silver Lake, Chip the Dam Builder . . .* my heart soared. This pushed me one step closer to being in a league with my teacher. Or so I felt. She began to explain to me that I would have a little catching up to do and that she would work with me on that. A vision of the two of us seated at a long library table strewn with books, papers, and pencils bubbled up in my head. We two, head to head, shoulder to shoulder. She would coach me. With her help, her little Olympian student would transform overnight into a third-grade wonder.

That night, as I floated home from school, I ignored the free yo-yo lessons offered in front of the corner grocery store on Admiral Way. I dreamed of showing Mrs. Parlato that she had chosen well. I would win every spelling bee and read out loud from books with never an *uh, er,* or mispronunciation. And yes, I would even stop bothering my neighbors. After all, I was being promoted. I would wear my new status as proudly as I did the blue velveteen dress my mother sewed for me. But I would never utter a word of this to Mrs. Parlato. She and I would simply share our secret sisterhood, silent recognition that we were on the same wavelength.

At dinner, my mother served what was customarily our Sunday meal. Fried chicken (a drumstick for me), mashed potatoes and gravy, canned green beans, and homemade chocolate pudding with whipped cream for dessert. She said we were celebrating my move to the third grade. Such attention and glory had me drifting high as a bright Chinese kite. Could life get any better? Even my father showed a level of pride in me that was unfamiliar. I was now definitely his little girl, made in his image, smart as a whip. Each high grade would earn me a dollar, he pronounced. Since I was out of teeth to lose for the tooth fairy and hated chores, this was a thrilling promise. My porcelain piggy bank would soon jingle.

Over the next few days in school, my classmates buzzed over my move. Somehow I was different to them. It felt as if I were wearing a Halloween mask, and no one could guess who I was. Except Mrs. Parlato.

What happened next changed everything. It started with my mother and the Avon lady. After serving percolated coffee and a plate-load of butter cookies to our neighbor-cum-cosmetics saleslady, Mother ordered a modest trio of facial cream, foundation, and lipstick. As a reward, she could pick two or three small sample lipsticks and try them out to see if, say, Startling Orange or Rumour of Red would become her next fashion color. I loved these little tubes. They piled up in a small silver tray on Mother's vanity. She never used them. They just sat there, waiting, pure potential.

I fiddled with the small plastic tubes in the tray after the Avon lady left, opening one to see what the color looked like. The first was pink, very pink, like the stiff net tutu on my Harriet Hubbard doll. Next, I opened another tube with a lipstick that was exactly like the deep red of Mrs. Parlato's lips. Quickly, I replaced the top, peeked in the vanity mirror to see if my mother was in sight, then stuffed the tiny tube into the pocket of my jumper. It was perfect. It was *our* red.

Lipstick tube under my pillow, I lay awake in my bed that night picturing my secret surprise for Mrs. Parlato. She would be astonished and pleased. She would nod at me with her dark eyes shining, just a single confirming nod. The next morning, I chose my clothes carefully. Yes to the blue corduroy skirt with the matching blue-and-gold plaid bolero. On the left side of the bolero, I pinned a small white plastic Pegasus that soared to the heavens. I lifted the small tube of lipstick from its hiding place under my pillow and stashed it in my skirt pocket.

When I arrived at the door of the portable, I took a deep breath and stepped toward my fate. First, a salute to the flag. Then roll call. Next, a continuation of our lessons on Japan. We were assigned to draw our versions of cherry blossom trees and Mt. Fujiyama. One boy planted an American flag on top of the legendary mountain. Another drew a plane with bombs falling like raindrops. The girl next to me struggled to draw a mountain. Hers looked more like an ice cream sundae. I drew thin trees dripping with pink blossoms, a Japanese lady with red lips walking beneath them, and snowcapped Fujiyama in the distance.

When the bell rang for morning recess, I slid out of my chair, stood up, and felt for the small tube in the lining of my pocket. Instead of rushing out with everyone else, I walked slowly to the door, ready to move ahead. I didn't play 7-Up, my favorite game, during recess. And I didn't talk with any of my friends. Instead I rushed into the girls' restroom in the main brick school building. It was empty. No one I knew would sacrifice a minute of play to go to the bathroom until just before the bell rang.

This gave me the time I needed. I looked straight at myself in the mirror and saw a tiny grownup staring back at me. I pursed my lips, eager to transform myself. Slowly, I applied lipstick as meticulously as I would paint within lines. When I finished, my lips glowed red, bright as Mrs. Parlato's. I would walk into the portable quietly, passing close by her desk as soon as the bell rang. I pictured the wide red smile on her face as she acknowledged my matching lips.

But the scene after the bell was nothing I imagined. The entire babbling class of students hushed the minute I walked into the portable, my red lips blazing. Instead of the wide approving smile I envisioned from Mrs. Parlato, her animated face froze into a stillness I had never seen. Her dark brows furrowed and her ripe, red lips stretched taut like a line. She rose slowly and seriously, then beckoned me to step outside the portable. "You'll have to wash those lips," she said softly, once we were out of earshot of the class. "Now. And you must never do this again." That was firm and final.

Where was the secret sisterhood? Where was the mutual recognition, silent but powerful? I was in an undertow, fighting not to be upended and swept beneath waves of shame.

⌒◎

Despite my fall from grace, Mrs. Parlato continued to give me creative assignments, send me home with new and advanced storybooks in my book

49

bag, praise my puppetry, and my gift with words. She even recommended to my parents that I be sent to a special drama program at Cornish School for the Arts for the summer. My father harrumphed at the thought of my getting any more crazy notions. "No goddamn acting for her," he growled. And that was it.

Each day in class, the gentle slap of reality Mrs. Parlato had delivered smarted less. But our eyes never again met in quite the same way. Where once I imagined affinity that knew no bounds, I now saw that she was merely this year's teacher, the tall dark-haired woman who stood at the front of the class as a leader for each of us. Never would she know the secrets of my heart, the longing I felt to become her handmaiden, her storyteller-in-waiting, her sister, her child. That smear of red lipstick I wore to signify our bond had failed its brilliant mission. Little did I realize that when I walked out of her classroom forever on a warm, sunny June day, I would carry the indelible mark of her lessons for life.

BERNESE BUDDHA

By: Tess Williams

When I first met a Bernese mountain dog at a party, I knew I had to have one of my own. This dog was a big fellow with a shiny black coat, fetching reddish-brown eyebrows, cheeks, and legs, and the softest white chest, forehead, and feet. As in a love story at the movies, everyone else seemed to disappear. I was captivated by the way his languorous mouth smiled as he nestled in close, confident that he was wanted.

On the way home, I whispered to my husband, "I hope that that can be our next dog."

Technically, it was my husband's turn to choose a dog breed. It was his beloved male German shepherd who had died several years earlier. So I was thrilled when he committed to the dog I loved. It meant more to me than roses or champagne. I had no idea though, that she would be as valuable to me as the sun.

The screening process we'd been through to be approved as worthy of a Bernese mountain dog was rigorous. We were asked if we both worked full time. No. Did we mind vacuuming? No. "Who besides you lives in the house?" We said, "Two small children and a ten-year-old golden retriever." I didn't mention that one of my children was troubled.

Once we had answered all the questions to the breeder's satisfaction, it was finally time to meet our long-awaited puppy. Five dreamy black, brown, and white fluff balls with chunky legs and fuzzy white feet greeted me. My heart turned up the Earth Wind and Fire tunes and danced, knowing that one of these Bernese mountain dog puppies was going to be mine.

I sat on the floor while the pups played around me. Their downy coats and clean, gamy smell contrasted with their sharp little teeth. Our family, having been the first to meet the breeder and commit to buying a puppy, was getting the pick of the litter, which was wonderful, but also overwhelming because at first it was hard to distinguish any individual characteristics. How would we choose? I was glad that on this first visit I was alone. I could settle in with them for a while and study the puppies' personalities. The truth was, this visit was a delicious respite from a challenging life—I was exhausted trying to find answers about how best to raise my troubled adopted son, Sacha.

Thoughts of home quickly drifted to the back of my mind when the largest puppy ambled over. He was called White Boy, named for an unusually large patch of white fur on his head, and he had a sweetness that made me think of that huge male, the first Bernese mountain dog I fell for, a lugubrious love hound.

All five of them were big flirts, darting back and forth between their droopy-eyed momma and me. No Collar Girl, distinguished from the other female puppy who wore a red collar, frequently came over to gaze into my eyes. She had a soulful intensity as if she were trying to tell me a secret, something essential.

On our second visit to see the puppies, I brought my family—my husband, our first-grade daughter, Julia, our kindergarten-age son, Sacha, and our golden retriever, Bula. The puppies were even fluffier than before. They tumbled about full of excitement to have visitors. Fixated on their pink paw pads and tiny whiskers, I still wondered, how would we choose? Again, No Collar Girl seemed to want to nestle in my lap and hold my gaze. She was calmer than most of them. We had been talking about getting a male, but there was no way to deny that I was smitten.

Bula, who seemed indifferent to the puppies, had been our "honeymoon baby." She was named Bula for the ebullient greeting on Fiji that we wanted to keep saying to remind us of a wonderful time and place. We loved Bula and now she was getting old. Part of the reason to get a puppy was to mitigate both the loss of our German shepherd and the anticipated loss of our Bula.

One of the males tickled my husband, John. A flirt and a trickster, this puppy liked to be chased and caught. John sat on the floor laughing, catching, and releasing the little guy.

I had to tell Sacha to "be gentle," and because he was often erratic, I kept a close eye on him as his sturdy hands restlessly moved from puppy to puppy. Sacha's developmental movement therapist had described his gait to be like a little bear that teetered side to side in order to move forward. At age five, Sacha didn't quite have a grip on how strong he was or how off balance. Neither did we.

We had adopted Sacha from Russia, a few months before his third birthday, believing he was a healthy child. When it became clear that he was not, we continually searched, and continue to search to this day, for various kinds of professional assistance to figure out how to help Sacha overcome behaviors we don't understand.

"Mommy, look I can pick them up, " said Julia.

Our children couldn't have been more different—unlike Sacha's, my daughter's touch was delicate and careful as if she were handling priceless antiques. Once when Julia was two and we were visiting a friend with exquisite Asian décor, I said to my friend, "Don't worry about anything breaking," and true to my word, Julia examined an object and put it down as gently as a feather landing on grass.

As I watched my children playing with the puppies, No Collar Girl decidedly sought me out and looked at me, tilting her head. Her eyes held the question, "Don't you see that I am yours and you are mine?" She followed my every movement. I was almost convinced that she was holding her breath until I looked back at her.

When it was time to leave and our host put the puppies back into their enclosure, the seemingly serene No Collar Girl hip-checked the competing male puppy out of the way as if to say, "These are my people. Go find your own." Our host concluded simply, "She chose you."

Driving home, I felt grateful to my husband. He had wanted a male but acknowledged that No Collar Girl emphatically decided she belonged with us. The kids were very excited, although they couldn't understand why we had to wait until she was eight weeks old before we could bring her home. During that long month while we got ready to pick up our puppy, I investigated Swiss names and ran them by the family. Ultimately, we choose the name "Greta," which means, "pearl." This name turned out to suit her more than we could have imagined.

Greta came home on Easter weekend. When we stopped the car on the way back to let her out to play, she stayed near us and did not try to run away as you might expect a little puppy to do. We liked being near her, too. Her tiny whiskers tickled our chins when we held her close.

At night, she slept in a crate and made little whooping noises that sounded just like a monkey, earning her the nickname "Monkey," which has stuck all of her life. I don't think she minded the crate as much as the physical separation from her people.

As she grew, we would go for walks, and when Greta got tired, she'd jump up on my legs to let me know she wanted to be carried. Eventually, Greta got too large and heavy—first for the kids and then for me to pick up, though she didn't know it. I hoped she didn't feel rejected since there wasn't any way to tell her, "You are just getting to be a very big girl."

Researching the breed, I learned that the Bernese mountain dog is an ancient lineage, part of the "working" classification of dogs. They were raised to be farm dogs and to pull carts of goat dairy products through the mountains of Switzerland. Their adult weight ranged from 80–130 pounds for an average dog. We bought a pack for Greta in anticipation of hiking together.

Bula eventually showed Greta the joy of swimming. It is not typical of a Bernese mountain dog to like water, but here was the influence of a golden retriever. I have a photograph of them at the beach when Greta was about six months old. Bula was joyfully splashing out to a stick we'd thrown as far as we could into the salty sea. I captured on film Greta's face, which showed: "Could I, should I, can I? I really want to!" and then she charged out, amazed at herself.

While Greta settled in, Sacha's behavior grew worse. I became a keen observer of my son, looking for his flattened eyes, his aggressively bitten nails, or small objects he'd broken. In turn, Greta became a keen observer of me. All it took was brief eye contact, and the very tip of her tail moved like the antenna of an insect finding its way. It wasn't long before both Greta and I came to understand how she was to be uniquely important to our family.

One afternoon, I picked Sacha up from school early. The principal had called to say, "Sacha has broken all of his pencils and when Mrs. White took them away, he came close to putting her eye out with one of the pieces."

At home, Sacha started banging his head on the wall. I had to hold him as he escalated into a full-blown rage. Greta witnessed all of this. She was not wagging her tail, but her eyes were kind. When I finally was able to get Sacha calmed down, Greta sat right next to me with her head, warm and re-assuring, in my lap. Trying to remain composed, I petted her soft, shiny fur.

Accustomed as I was to outwardly holding a calm space for Sacha, Greta, by now a full-grown, eighty-five-pound dog, was not fooled for a minute. She clearly intuited my trembling heart and stayed near me, somehow affirming that I was doing the right thing.

Watching Sacha with Greta, I was deeply relieved to see that he did not want to harm her. Greta was not afraid of him. In fact, Greta often lay down on the floor belly up, waggling her legs and looking at us tenderly. Her greatest wish was to please us.

Even during meal times, which could be trying at our house, Greta brought a sense of restraint and serenity. Most dogs love to eat and many American dogs are overweight, but Greta has always been a dainty eater who never learned the "clean your plate" rule of her species. She never finished the last few pieces of kibble in her bowl. By contrast, Sacha ate like a starving wolf with no interest in the conversation or the family norms of keeping our mouths closed while we chew or using our napkins. Sacha's lack of manners made my husband so tense that sometimes I felt the air would explode. Greta sat behind my chair during meals as if to give me a current of calm from which I could feed my family.

Greta extended that sense of calm to her fellow dogs as well. She had gone to puppy kindergarten to learn basic commands although, truth be told, it was more about teaching us, especially the kids, how to interact with her. She was so eager to please that she became the puppy who was paired with skittish or aggressive dogs for training exercises. Eventually, she advanced to Paws for Reading, a program designed to encourage struggling readers through the nonjudgmental interest of a dog.

Reading out loud, we learned, was one of the best ways for a child to develop brain circuits. Since Greta's experience in Paws for Reading was so positive, we decided to get her certified as a therapy dog. This enabled Sacha to proudly have his popular pet in the classroom. The children were thrilled to have Greta sit next to them when it was their turn to read. She would wag and look at them with as much attention as if they were offering her steak and lobster. To this day, students will come up to me and say, "I knew Greta when I was little. She's the best dog ever!"

When people asked how we trained her to become a therapy dog, I said, "We didn't—we simply put her through the tests. This is just the way she is." For one of the seven tests that she had to pass, Greta and I walked through a field of clanging garbage can lids, clattering wheelchairs, squeaky walkers, loud music, other dogs, and tight spaces. She strolled along, smiling her Bernese smile as if it was the most fun she'd had in years.

When we walked together in town to do our errands, she would receive a wave of adulation. At the bank, the tellers would say, "I need some therapy today—please come to my window." Greta would run right over to them, sit courteously on her tail, and lean reassuringly back into their legs, tilting her head up to look at them while they were petting her. As someone who values community and harmonious interpersonal relationships, this gave me a lift so needed after being the outcast in the playground with the boy everyone avoided.

At the gym, as I attached her leash to the outdoor bench near the other dogs, the people at the front desk would ask, "Can't she be here with us?" They'd all snap pictures with their phones when she'd rub her paws over her eyes while peeking up at them.

True, she is a beautiful animal; her father was in fact a top show dog, but it is something else that draws everyone. She gives off an energetic aura of loving kindness and compassion that people want to touch; the way they touch the hands or feet of their spiritual teachers or the cheek of a newborn baby.

Greta's wagging tail is the metronome of our family's well-being. She follows me with her eyes and calmly asks permission: "Can I go in this door? Can I eat this now? Should I wait? Can I join the group now?" Only when we are traveling and away from her too long, or the stress too high within her pack, does she develop a hot-spot skin condition. It is her way of showing that she absorbed the stress into her own body, and yet she still gives out love. Greta is ecstatic whenever I come in the front door. She likes me to sit on the bench and she snuggles back into my legs without breaking her gaze while I hug her and stroke the whitest, softest fur on her chest.

There have been times when I have been unable to sleep, when I spent a good portion of each day shaking with fear, exhaustion, and the entrapment inherent in raising my mentally ill son. I am an extrovert who had once enjoyed a vibrant career, who had once delighted in playgroups and the company of other moms with my charming little girl. But that all changed when Sacha came along. Sure, kickboxing, yoga, and the support of my husband helped, but it was my constant companion, my self-selected, gorgeous sweetheart, with the brown freckle on her white nose that saved me from despair and the isolation of raising a son who no one wanted their child to be around.

At fifteen, Sacha is now going to a special ranch school in the Southwest, and I finally have time to take care of myself. I joined a writing group chosen in part because the teacher is an environmentalist and an animal lover. Knowing she would be a contribution to the group, I asked if it would be okay to bring Greta. Naturally, the teacher said, "yes."

Greta is always thrilled to come. She often sits near my chair, but she periodically makes the rounds and is especially attuned to anyone who is sharing something emotional. Greta will often go near them and be attentive. Many a member of our group, scratching behind Greta's ears and petting her coat, still glossy at age nine, says, "I feel better already."

As it turned out, Greta not only became a certified therapy dog capable of helping out in the world of schools, nursing homes, and hospitals, but she also proved to be more valuable to our family than any therapist, doctor, or educator. She is the magical glue that holds us together with her blameless love.

One day my writing group did an exercise to see where we were on the continuum of wisdom found after much life experience. The nine of us arranged ourselves in a half circle. Our venerable Japanese elder stood the farthest along the path of wisdom. Greta, without a moment's hesitation, placed herself squarely, not at my feet, but on the feet of our elder member. Greta leaned as close as she could to her and looked into her eyes to say, "You and I belong here."

To say Greta helped us during the years Sacha was home is an understatement. She was a role model of steadiness for a volatile boy and was my private counterforce, helping me to survive extreme trauma. Like the gem she is named after, the constant irritation and stress of life polished Greta's natural gifts until she was precious—my elder pearl.

SO, DO YOU HAVE ANY BROTHERS OR SISTERS?

By: Lizbeth Anne Adams

"**S**o, do you have any brothers or sisters?" was a question that always troubled me.

This time, the question came from Dale, the laboratory technician. We were both seated in front of microtomes, instruments used to make very thin slices of preserved tissue for biochemical analysis. Dale turned his face slightly toward me while keeping his eyes on his slices.

I froze. This perfectly innocuous question always felt like a punch to my gut. When people asked about my siblings, I generally tried to keep my answer short: "I have a brother." Invariably, the following question would be, "Oh, and what does he do?" or "And where does he live?" I loved my brother and I missed him, and I didn't know where he was. I was ashamed there was mental illness in my family. I was afraid people would think less of me if they knew.

I had earned my PhD, and was doing a post-doctoral fellowship in a well-respected lab at the University of Washington. I had already garnered prestigious awards and accolades on my path to an academic research career. I worked hard to convince people I had a good mind, and it was important to me that nothing changed their perceptions.

When people pressed for more information about my brother, I couldn't say, "He's a brilliant musician, making a living as a singer," or "He and his family live right here in town," or any of the things I should reasonably have been able to say about John, had fate been kinder to him. So I generally said, "Well, I'm not really sure where he is at the moment," and then did everything in my power to steer the conversation in a different direction.

I hated myself for that. Every single time, I felt like Judas. But to keep my own image burnished bright, I felt I needed to avoid talking about my mentally ill brother. I believed that my career and my intelligence were the life raft that would keep my young son and me afloat, even as the rest of my family was disintegrating.

But on that day in the lab, something about Dale's kind voice and genuine interest penetrated my carapace.

"I have a brother," I said hesitantly. "I'm not sure where he is, though. My family hasn't heard from him for over a year."

"Does he travel a lot?" Dale asked conversationally, innocently.

"I guess you could say that," I responded. "He's, um, he's not well. He's had a hard time finding himself."

Dale must have heard the stress in my voice—he turned to look at me more fully. I met his eyes, warm and brown, set in a cheerful face underneath a receding hairline. His was a face that put people at ease.

"Happens to the best of us," he said, smiling kindly at me.

The best of us, yes. Something about that phrase triggered my honest grief.

"Actually, Dale, he's mentally ill. He's schizophrenic, and my family doesn't know where he is. He was the smartest, nicest, most talented person, and I'm not just saying that because he's my brother." I smiled wanly as I tried to defend my objectivity, my rational mind. Dale's expression was empathetic, free of disgust or rejection.

"He graduated from college with a degree in physics. He was so smart," I repeated. "It was awful to watch his mind start to fail him. I could tell that he knew something terrible was happening, and none of us knew how to help him. We don't know where he is. We don't even know if he's alright."

Tears began to slide down my cheeks, right there in public, right there in the lab. Dale's expression softened even further. He and his wife had adopted a daughter who turned out to have severe developmental problems, and I knew he too had suffered over the unexpected condition of a loved one. Maybe that was why I was able to open up to him.

"Liz, I'm really sorry to hear this. I know how your family must agonize over him. Schizophrenia is a bad illness, from what I know of it. But maybe someone here, or at some other university, will start figuring out some ways to treat it," Dale said. He too wanted to believe in science. "I hope he comes home soon." Dale touched my shoulder lightly, then nodded to indicate he was turning back to his work.

Yes, my family agonized as we each tried to plot a course through this uncharted territory of a loved one's madness. I struggled to build the life I envisioned for myself: educated, with a career and a family of my own. At times, I defended that vision too vigorously. What I did not tell Dale that day was the story of the dinner party I'd held ten years prior.

John was not yet flagrantly ill, but he was clearly not well. My family told others and ourselves that he was "going through a rough patch," "not yet living his potential," and "still trying to find himself." John and I got together for lunches, dinners, movies, and coffee, but it was increasingly apparent that he was drifting farther from normal behavior and cognition.

Just a year or so into my graduate schoolwork, I decided to have a dinner party for two other couples from the lab, plus my husband and me. It would be the first time any of them had come to our house, and I wanted them to be impressed with me, not only as a budding scientist, but also as a hostess and cook. In retrospect, I see all the emotional issues with which I burdened this dinner: my profound sense of inadequacy and legacies from my mother that included a crippling fear of entertaining and a certainty of quick and harsh judgment.

Manifesting my own version of insanity, I prepared to host this party. I cleaned the house for days and days, scrubbing baseboards and deep-cleaning the linen closets, since dinner guests, we know, always explore the dark recesses of other people's cupboards. They would find no hidden dirt in mine. Although I had no experience cooking Indian food, I planned an elaborate Indian meal. I carefully decorated the house, cutting rhododendrons from the yard that complemented the Indian bedspread I used as a tablecloth. In a state of acute anxiety, I worked myself to exhaustion.

The night of the party arrived. Each of the many dishes I planned to prepare was complicated, comprising long lists of ingredients and spices, which I meticulously measured out in advance. Plates of chopped vegetables and meats crowded together with tiny bowls holding mounds of asafetida, turmeric, ginger, cinnamon, and other pungent powders on my kitchen counters. The assembly of this meal required complex timed cooking steps, and I was laboring to finalize the flow chart of what was to be added to what dish when the phone rang.

"Hello?" I said abruptly, frazzled. I hoped for a moment that people were calling to cancel.

"Liz? What's up, seester? You sound like a flea on a griddle."

John's voice, familiar as my own breath, was not one I wanted to hear at this moment. His whimsical turns of phrase, so often charming, now set off warning bells. The scientists due to arrive any minute would know that flea sounds are inaudible, on or off griddles.

Why was he calling? Did he need a ride somewhere? Was he in trouble? Did he want to come over? He didn't sound upset, but his life had become so unpredictable that one never knew what kind of shape he was in. I could feel the muscles in my neck tightening as I waited for his next words. An image flashed into my mind of John showing up at the door an hour hence, unkempt, unbathed, and sitting down at my carefully staged dinner table. I saw my colleagues listening to his verbal flights of fancy, exchanging puzzled glances with each other, and then turning to regard me with concern. Heat began to creep up my face.

"John, I can't talk right now. I'm right in the middle of something." I spoke too loudly, too forcefully. Too cruelly.

"Liz, no. Wait . . . " John's voice was a receding Doppler as I moved the receiver from my ear to the hard black cradle of the phone. There was the clunk of plastic on plastic, and then silence.

Now thirty years later, I don't even remember how the dinner party went. I imagine that my anxiety suffused its flavor into the food we ate. But I do remember how I treated my brother, how I denied him. Remorse stabs me deeply every time I recall that night, and shame sears my spine. If I had the chance again, I would leave a note on the front door, telling people to let themselves in, make themselves comfortable, and check out the linen closets. I would go pick up my brother, bring him to my table, and encourage the expressions of his beautiful mind. I would stand right beside him. I would not hide him. Would it have changed John's fate?

As the years progressed, my brother made no turnarounds. By the time of my teary conversation with Dale, John had been in and out of hospitals and institutions, arrested for petty crimes, and lived much of his life on the streets. My parents exhausted themselves and their resources trying to get help for him. As I struggled to keep my own life afloat and as John got sicker and sicker, it became harder for me to be around him. I was terrified at the thought that looking at him, I might be looking into a mirror.

~⚬

In the aftermath of my life unspooling through a long and painful divorce, I moved into a peaceful little cottage on Thornton Creek, near the shores of Lake Washington. I showed John my new house on a warm summer evening when my son, Chase, was with his dad. We sat with our cups of coffee on a wooden bench by the creek and watched a kingfisher dart from tree to tree. My new German shepherd puppy sat next to me, his chest against my knee. Maintaining a watchful guard, his eyes moved between my face and John's.

"Nice place, seester," John said.

He was pretty quiet and seemed calm. In moments like this, my mind leapt ahead to the day when he would be well. If he could just hang on, someone would find the right medication, even a cure. I never gave up that hope. What I did not know, as we sat there in companionable silence, was that this was the last time I would ever see him.

"Yep, it is. I couldn't have done it without Dad. He always tries to help us, doesn't he, John?" I looked over at my brother, wanting to remind him how much he and I were loved.

John nodded, silent.

"The whole divorce thing was pretty unpleasant," I continued. "There were times when I just wanted to give up. But I have to stick around for Chase. He'd miss me if I checked out."

What was I saying? I had never seriously thought about "checking out," dreadful as some days had been during my marriage and its dissolution. Was I begging John to hold on? His life was so much harder than mine, and though I did not know if he had, it would not have surprised me if he thought about ending the pain.

"I guess lots of people would miss you, Liz," John said, sadness in his voice.

At the time, I wasn't quite certain what he meant by this, but I can only imagine how John, so long beloved, so deeply admired when he was healthy, felt utterly alone as he drifted in and out of madness. We didn't know where he went, those times he disappeared. We didn't know for sure that he didn't have friends somewhere, but it seemed unlikely. He was living alone with my father, unable to work, unable to play much music, unable to have the life he deserved. He didn't sound angry at me, that I had ended up with a life that, however flawed, was much closer to the life he should have had.

If I had known that this was my last chance to talk to him, what would I have said? I would have entreated him to stay, not to hit the road again. I would have poured out my love for him, my admiration for his talents, my sorrow at his ill luck to be struck with this disease. I would have begged his forgiveness for ever keeping him a secret. Mostly, I would have thanked him for saving my life. Not all of my good fortune can be attributed to him, but what is true is this: Because of John, I stayed alive and healthy enough to enjoy my good fortune. What is true is that John protected me against my mom's anger, against neighborhood bullies, against physical illness, against being the uncool new kid in so many schools, against loneliness. What is true is that John gave me my deepest connection to music, my deepest earliest friendship, my deepest trust. John gave me the things I still treasure most.

I did not know, as we sat there, that soon he would leave our parents' house for the last time, in the late summer of 1993. It would be many, many years before my father could tell me the story of John's final night at home. I would come to learn that Dad blamed himself for John's leaving, which became a grief and a guilt that bore down on my dad, periodically stopping his heart.

Dad was John's sole caregiver and spent his days trying to both care for and entertain my brother. On occasion, more frequently as John's illness progressed, Dad would show up with a cut above his eye or a bruise on his cheek. I would ask him what happened and he'd always say, "Oh, I ran into a door," or "A tree branch snapped back when I was pruning it." I didn't want to believe that John was capable of violence against my dad. Once I asked him pointblank: "Daddy, is John hurting you?" My father gave me a look that informed me that he would never tell me, and that I was never to ask again. "No, of course not," he replied gruffly.

On John's last day at home, he and Dad decided to take a road trip to Canada, a few hours north by car. As Dad later reported it, when they got to the border, John became belligerent toward the patrol, and both he and my dad were taken into a back room and searched and then were refused entry into Canada. My father was the most rule-abiding person I knew—this caused him complete mortification.

"I got mad at him," he said to me, when he could finally bring himself to talk about it. His voice was cracking, and his eyes were red-rimmed, he who never cried. "I got mad at him for getting us into trouble. I drove way too fast on the way home. He saw that I was mad."

"Oh, Dad," I pleaded. "Please don't beat up on yourself. No one on this planet worked as hard as you did to take care of John. John knew how much you loved him. He wasn't in his right mind, but I know he felt your love."

Dad struggled to compose himself. "When we got back home, we hadn't eaten and tried to go to Roberto's to get some pizza. But they wouldn't let us in. Evidently, John had caused some trouble there, and they turned us away at the door. The next morning he was gone."

"Dad, it wasn't your fault. John was sick and often didn't know what he was doing, or if he did, he couldn't control it. Maybe he left to try to protect us."

I was to learn later that this is not unusual. Schizophrenics, so often intelligent and creative, suffer from a disease of the mind, not the heart. When they see the pain they are causing their loved ones, they may choose to remove themselves to spare others the pain of their own illness. John was sometimes able to control his disease, but more and more frequently it was jerking him around like a marionette. I imagine he was ashamed that he had caused my father distress and embarrassment. I imagine that his good heart bade him leave.

But all this was still in the future that day as John and I sat by the creek. I rubbed my puppy's ears as I told my brother about the things I wanted to do with the house and the yard.

"Maybe we can work on some of this stuff together, if you want," I said. "You've got such a great eye for color. What color do you think I should paint the outside?"

"Blue. It's your favorite, right?"

We talked as the sun dipped lower over the creek. I offered to give him a ride back to our parents' house, but he said he wanted to take the bus, that he might stop off downtown. He stood up, dusting off the seat of his pants. He looked at me, neither of us knowing.

"See ya," he said, and in his last act of protection, he left for good.

I watched him walk away. There was still grace in his gait. His long brown hair caught the last rays of the day's sun.

THE UNSPEAKABLE

By: Donna James

Any stranger listening at the memorial would have thought Mark had died falling in a climb "doing what he loved best," as people like to say, or that he had peacefully passed surrounded by intimate family and friends after a brief, fatal illness. A hundred people looked out over a serene wooded hillside through a wall of windows. But Carolyn was too shocked by the denial surrounding her client's death to enjoy the view. Everyone there knew that Mark had committed suicide. Everyone must have whispered about it, felt the sudden collapse of space in the mind and heart that follows such news. But there was no hint of this shadow at the service.

Carolyn had been grieving the loss of her client for a couple of months. Mark had been with her for only twelve sessions over even fewer weeks. As one of her psychotherapy colleagues consoled her, "He hardly even gave you a chance."

Mark had conducted three in-person interviews with therapists, including Carolyn. Several days after his meeting with her, he called for an appointment. He arrived with Marianne, his aunt, a woman in her mid-thirties, only a few years older than he. She insisted that Mark tell Carolyn what he had done.

With his eyes downcast, he began. "It was the day after I saw you. I've had the idea for a long time . . . I had to try it. I moved the car into the garage and pulled the door down. There was a long plastic tube I'd been keeping on the shelf. I shoved it up the tailpipe and snaked the other end through the window. Then I got in the car and turned it on. And the CD player. I wanted to listen to "Knockin' On Heaven's Door." I remember playing it over and over. Then I don't remember anything. My roommate found me lying in the driveway."

They sat, silent. Marianne broke the spell. "You're the therapist he felt comfortable with. He says you've worked with a lot of suicidal people and depression is your specialty. He needs your help. Will you work with him?"

Carolyn studied Mark, his close-cropped curly brown hair, the well-groomed and tidy appearance of his slight but rugged body. He looked like a man who took pride in staying fit. His was not the kind of depression that kept him planted in bed. He was interesting, unusual.

Carolyn asked Mark crucial questions about his life, his depression, his suicidal thoughts. She listened to his story not only with her ears but with her body. As with most new clients, she took him in whole, getting to know his interior through her own interior. For Carolyn this was an important way of knowing people. It gave her an empathic route into the heart of the problem. After integrating this information in the first session or two, she would relax into letting clients teach her their own troubled interpretations of themselves.

"Psychotherapy can't begin until you stop using," Carolyn insisted. "I think you need inpatient treatment. And a psychiatrist to prescribe antidepressants. When that's done, call me and we'll set up a regular time to meet."

Mark, watchful, looked up at her from his slouch. He straightened himself and met her calm attentive eyes, a slight crease in his brow.

"You think I have a drug problem." He restated her position as though he questioned her reasoning.

"I think you're self-medicating your depression. And it's not working," Carolyn clarified.

Mark held her gaze as he contemplated her comments. She waited, sure of her stance, honed with years of practice, wondering if he would accept her assessment. She was pleased when he finally responded.

"Alright, that makes sense to me. How do I do this?"

Carolyn detected a subtle shift in Mark that boded well for their work together. She recommended several treatment centers. Marianne agreed to help him negotiate the arrangements and hold his feet to the fire.

Eight weeks later he called for an appointment. "I'm back from treatment. When can I come in?"

Carolyn heard the eager energy in his voice. She made time for him the following day.

Mark laid out for Carolyn the insights he'd had about himself during therapy in the treatment center.

"All my life, I've looked in the mirror and seen this ugly little troll. I've never been attractive to women. But maybe it has more to do with how I feel about myself than how anybody else sees me," he said. "I think you were right about my using marijuana and alcohol, and sometimes coke, to keep myself from getting depressed. I don't need them with these antidepressants."

Before leaving her office, Mark handed Carolyn a list of his medications. "I need to find a shrink to prescribe meds. The guy at Westfield put me on these."

Carolyn gave him a few names. "By the way, what's become of that plastic pipe you used a few months back?"

"Marianne threw it out," he replied, making his way quickly toward the door without looking back at her.

They met twice a week. Mark's suicidal thoughts were always at the forefront. He never failed to assure her he would not act on them. Still, she didn't have faith that he knew himself well enough to make such a promise. Every time he left her office, Carolyn wondered if she would see him again. Five weeks into treatment, she went on a long-planned vacation. Mark declined to meet with the colleague who was covering for her. He agreed to contact his new psychiatrist in an emergency, a verbal contract with Carolyn that he would fail to uphold.

Carolyn came to the memorial to put to rest her grief over Mark's loss. He *hadn't* given her a chance. She hoped that sitting among other people who were grieving for him would help her understand why the bond she had tried to establish had not been strong enough to hold on to him.

She purposely arrived late; if she came in during the formal part of the service, she would be saved the awkwardness of not being free to explain to anyone who she was and how she knew Mark. It would be a breach of confidentiality to divulge it, even after his death. But this gathering had been planned to allow people to mingle and talk. As she arrived, Carolyn could overhear reconnections and new introductions being made across Mark's different circles. So when she slipped into a chair in the back row, it was no more than a minute before she was accosted by the very question she had tried to avoid.

"How did you know Mark?" asked the kind-faced, middle-aged man sitting beside her.

"Professionally," she stammered, then abruptly excused herself and made her way toward Marianne. Carolyn had spotted the unmistakable curly hair atop the small frame of the woman she had met only once.

"Marianne, do you remember me? I'm Carolyn, Mark's therapist," she spoke softly.

"Oh, yes. I'm so glad you decided to be with us."

"I feel a little out of place, Marianne. People want to know how I knew Mark. I think you're his closest relative here. I'd feel better if I had your permission to tell them I was his therapist."

"Certainly, say whatever you want. I don't think he would mind."

Returning to her seat in the back row, Carolyn fell again into conversation with her inquisitive neighbor. She explained that she had needed to ask Mark's relatives if they objected to her identifying herself; she revealed that she had been his therapist for a brief time before he died.

The man leaned toward her, for the first time looking at her closely. "It must have been difficult for you."

Disturbing emotions stirred in Carolyn. She knew that people expect therapists to keep clients alive. What, she wondered, did he imagine she would feel when a client committed suicide on her watch? Did he suspect the anger, self-doubt, the slap to the ego that most therapists feel when a client leaves them like that? Did he think Mark's suicide was her failure? She had sometimes felt unspoken criticism, even from people in her own profession, when she talked about having experienced client suicides.

"Yes, and still is sometimes," Carolyn confessed.

They were interrupted by a man at the front of the room announcing, "Please, everybody, come and take a seat." He waited for the crowd to settle into their chairs.

"Welcome everyone. I'm Jeff Sorenson. Mark and I were at the U Dub together back in the day. Four of us rented a house. That was a *reeeally* long *partay!* I probably don't have to tell you Mark was usually the life of that party. The instigator. A terrific fun guy."

Jeff invited people to come to the open space up front to tell their stories about Mark. One by one, people took the floor, reminiscing about good times, expounding on Mark's practical jokes and outrageous puns. A colleague who had been away cycling in Switzerland for a month recalled that when he approached his desk on his first day back, he found a bicycle seat mounted on the casters that once rolled his office chair. Curious, Carolyn listened to stories of Mark's social world.

As the funny, touching flashbacks from Mark's life accumulated, Carolyn felt an irritation welling up, her stomach tightening, and her mind wanting to disconnect from her body. Nobody was saying a word about a side of Mark that had been the main focus of her work with him. She had not expected the service to be a therapy session; she understood that the bereaved needed to make peace with Mark's death. They were not there to analyze how an athlete with a master's degree and many adoring friends could, for the second time, idle his car in a closed garage and, this time, wait to die. Still, was it possible that a hundred people could sit there knowing what they all knew without even an intimation of his troubled psyche? Did they intend to bury that part of Mark with him? Had they truly known him?

The funny stories, so disconnected from her own experience of Mark, horrified and overwhelmed Carolyn. She felt herself filling up with some substance she could not name, that she couldn't even call her own, as though she were becoming possessed by an alien presence. Could this be how Mark had felt, she wondered, as his lungs filled with carbon monoxide? Her mind twitched along with her body. All of sudden, she was taken onto her feet as though a hand were gripping the front of her dress and propelling her out of her chair and across the room. She looked into the expectant faces before her.

"I was Mark's therapist for two months just before he died." Carolyn was astounded to hear her own voice. "He had a dark side . . . I was privileged to see it . . . and spend time with it."

She went quiet for a long moment and then blurted out again, "He had a dark side!" It was less an announcement than a plea.

As Carolyn threaded her way back to her seat, mute faces turned away from her. Even her friendly neighbor averted his eyes. She could not think to search for Marianne's face in the crowd. She felt like she was moving through dense translucent particles of silence, clear and clean as crystals.

Finally, a man got up and said, "Whew! It's heavy in here." A twitter of relieved laughter spread through the room. Then he told the story of Mark calling him at three in the morning instructing him to get to his TV fast. *Dead Men Don't Wear Plaid* was on, and Mark wanted to know that somebody else was up in the middle of the night watching it with him, even if it was across town. There were smiles of acknowledgment, chuckling.

Carolyn could feel the space between her and everyone else widen as the tales of "Mark the Card" went on. Finally, enough stories told, the crowd moved out into the park behind the building where they walked together to watch the planting of a tree in Mark's memory. Around Carolyn, an empty circle six feet in diameter formed, a zone of contagion that not one person would enter, even in the tight squeeze along the wooded path that led to the site of the planting. The space contorted its shape to accommodate a safe quarantine from her.

But Carolyn had a gnawing sensation that she was not alone in that cell. She could feel Mark in there with her, tucked securely into the bubble created by her revelation. In Carolyn's mind, he had assigned her the task of unburdening him of the message he had not felt permitted to deliver himself. Now, she was experiencing *with him* the isolation that she imagined he feared if he had told his friend why he was up in the middle of the night watching an old movie.

Carolyn couldn't fathom that some of these people at Mark's memorial had not themselves spent a restless night after he died, wondering what they hadn't noticed, how they might have been different with him, just as she had. Surely, some of them had been shaken, sickened even, by his violent death. But it seemed to Carolyn that, on this day, there was an implicit rule that this was to be a celebration with no regrets, no bad feelings, no real grief. Everyone would keep Mark's secret. But no one had sent that directive to Carolyn. The message to *her* was from Mark himself. He had agitated her insides, stirred a craziness that grabbed her there in the back row and forced her to speak what he himself had held for so many years.

As the tree was planted, Carolyn felt shunned. This profound isolation produced in her a sudden belief that she was irretrievably bad. It felt like she had broken a social imperative, saying the most inappropriate thing possible. She wondered if she had also broken with professional conduct;

she had said more than a therapist ought to say about a client. And in public. That she had felt eerily compelled to tell Mark's secret and had been given permission to "say whatever you want," did not give her the right to declare his private black hole to the world. Permission did not relieve her of guilt and shame. Carolyn felt she should have restrained herself, held the urge within instead of acting it out.

Now it was not Mark who possessed her so much as these dark, loathsome feelings castigating her for her sin. Her rational self would know this punishment far exceeded the level of her crime. But in her collapsed state of mind, she *felt* she deserved it.

On the way to her car, Carolyn saw Marianne in the parking lot and approached her once again.

"I'm so sorry," she lamented. "I didn't mean for that to happen. But nobody else was saying it."

"Well," Marianne replied, shrugging her shoulders, seeming unfazed, "that *is* the other side of it." Perhaps Marianne had endured enough of Mark's depression and was content, now, to let it go.

It was not until the drive home that Carolyn was able to wrench herself out of the pain and reclaim her own core. Feeling like herself again, she remembered the "sin-eaters" of the old tradition in the British Isles who were called to a house where someone had died. Such a person took upon himself eating from a bowl of food placed on the body of the deceased, thus magically taking on the person's sins so the soul could go to the afterlife in peace. Sin-eaters, too, were shunned, living apart until called to perform their function.

Carolyn had felt Mark taking over her body. Yet her clinician self understood the way people's actions beget reactions in others. She remembered times in the consulting room when she had felt possessed by something that did not seem to have originated within herself. Had she not felt possessed by Mark, she would not have told "the other side of it" out loud, as Marianne had called it. Without having done that deed, she would not have felt such gnawing mental and emotional distress. Mark's message was not only a communication to his community through her. It was a message that was directed at her own heart.

Empathy was not enough; she had been required to experience the emotional miasma from which suicide rises. Perhaps Mark, even beyond the grave, needed someone to feel what he had felt—to utter the unspeakable—in order to rest peacefully. In this primal, intimate last transmission, perhaps Mark *had* given her a chance.

GREAT EXPECTATIONS

By: Meredith Bailey

As Angie Meyer drummed her fingers on the cash register at DrugMart, she thought about two things: how much she wanted a cigarette and how badly she wanted to tell Paul about the letter in her pocket. But because she couldn't tell him, she hadn't told anyone. In fact, Angie had nearly forgotten she'd taken the SATs until the letter with her score arrived in yesterday's mail.

As she reached into her pocket to confirm she hadn't dreamed the letter's existence, a girl not much older than Angie dumped baby wipes and foot powder on the counter. A towheaded little boy wandered in circles around her legs. This girl was like so many teenagers in Pocomoke who got pregnant and never made it out. *This is the kind of future everyone imagines when they look at me,* Angie thought.

"Hello?" the girl snapped. "I don't have all day."

"Of course not. Your total's $7.32," Angie replied crisply, plastering on her fake customer-service grin.

It didn't seem like a mouth should be able to stretch so wide on such a small, angular face. At seventeen, Angie was pretty, but she didn't want to be, so she masked her natural beauty with layers of black eyeliner, red streaks in her mahogany hair, grubby jeans, and a thin silver-studded dog collar around her neck.

The girl glared at Angie as she fumbled with her wallet, her son now pointing at the candy bars and begging.

"No Toby—put that back," his mother fumed. "You know better!"

The girl's words to her son softened Angie. *You know better,* meaning, you should act better. I expect better from you. Angie wished that someone in her own family had expected more of her.

After the girl paid, Angie pulled the paper from her pocket, the letter proclaiming her 1450 SAT score. Then she let out an acerbic chuckle—a near perfect score didn't mean much to someone who had been expelled from school, did it?

Angie imagined everyone had been relieved when she'd been kicked out. She was just one of many Meyers who had been expelled, arrested, addicted, or knocked up too young. When you lived in a town like this, you were supposed to live up to your name—good or bad—so it unnerved teachers and peers when she qualified for AP classes, and then got Cs, sometimes Bs, without doing any of the work.

When Angie told her mother she'd been expelled from Pocomoke High, her mother had shrugged and lit a cigarette from the pilot light on the stove.

"Want one?" she had asked.

"No," Angie shot back. "Did you hear what I said?"

"What do you want me to say? That it's a shame? It's not like you were going to be a rocket scientist or anything," her mother had said, blowing smoke out of the corner of her mouth. "You can clean houses with me. You don't need a diploma for that."

Angie understood her mother wasn't trying to be hurtful—just realistic. She knew nothing about Angie's academic life, about the books she stayed up late reading in her room, about the extra calculus problems she did in class for no other reason than to quell her boredom.

"Excuse me, can I pay for these?" a woman asked tentatively, putting her items on the counter.

When Angie looked up, she went pale. She had been wondering when this moment would happen and what she would do when it did. Before her, in a pink-and-white-striped maternity sundress, stood the real reason for her expulsion from school. Before her stood Paul's wife.

"Sure," Angie muttered, stuffing the letter back in her pocket. As she rang up moisturizer and nail polish remover, Angie stole glances at the woman. Her name was Joanna. Angie had never seen her up close before, suddenly realizing, apart from the age difference, how similar they looked. Joanna was short, and probably petite when she wasn't pregnant, with long brown hair—a shade lighter than Angie's—and dark eyes.

"Gorgeous day, isn't it?" Joanna remarked, gazing out the window behind the cash register.

"Yep," Angie replied, pausing as she stared at a package of Irish Spring soap. She nearly laughed out loud—*that* was what he smelled like, that was the fresh, aloe scent she'd breathed in when she had kissed that hollow in his neck, right below his ear. Angie had assumed it was some kind of cologne, but no, just soap his wife had bought for him.

"Miss, I'm in a bit of a hurry—have a doctor's appointment to get to," Joanna said, rubbing her round belly.

"Sure, sorry." Angie gritted her teeth. The woman was blithely staring out the window at the bright June sun with no idea that Angie could rip apart her perfect life in a second. She had been dreaming about this day—had gleefully imagined the look of horror on this woman's face as she stocked shelves and repeated, "Have a nice day" ad nauseam.

"I'll take this, too," Joanna said, setting a package of spearmint gum on the counter. "My husband's trying to quit smoking. Seems to help."

Since when, Angie thought to herself, recalling their pre-coital cigarettes. He'd always wanted to share one with her before, not after. When Joanna opened her wallet, Angie's heart stilled. There was a picture of Paul, her AP English teacher. There were his gentle blue eyes and his slightly perplexed smile, the same expression he'd had on his face the day he'd returned her very first essay with a D. She still took it out of her nightstand, reread the daring message scribbled in bright green cursive at the top: *Half-assed job! You can do better than this.* No other teacher—hell, no one else in her whole life—had ever noticed her lack of effort before.

Angie stared at Paul's picture as she continued ringing up his wife's items. Unlike Joanna, Paul wasn't attractive. He was short, with a receding hairline, and was thick around the middle. He wore ugly ties, often coffee-stained, that didn't match his shirts. But his appearance had been irrelevant to Angie. What mattered was the way he looked at her. The expectation in his eyes that she had something interesting to say.

A few months ago, he would have been the one she told about her SAT score. He would have hugged her, whispered in her ear what he always said, "You're destined for great things, my dear." Angie looked up at his wife, whose lips were pursed with impatience, and wondered what he murmured to her when he held her close.

"Miss, are you okay?" Joanna asked.

"Yes, I just, I'm sorry—this doesn't seem to be ringing up," Angie lied, holding the Irish Spring. "I'll have someone do a price check." She waved a fellow employee over and handed him the soap, explaining what she needed.

Joanna sighed and looked at her watch. "I need to be on my way. Maybe I should just leave it . . ."

"Really, it will just take a second," Angie said, desperately trying to think of something else to say. She couldn't let her leave. Not yet. As much as she hated this woman, she was the only connection to Paul that Angie had now. "So . . . how far along are you?"

"Twenty-six weeks," Joanna said, her smile returning. "This is our first."

Angie did the calculation in her head—twenty-six weeks was about six months. What had she and Paul been doing six months ago today? Had he fooled around with her after school in the back of his blue Buick and then gone home to make a baby with his wife?

"Well, congratulations," Angie said, her tone turning caustic. "How exciting." The more she thought about it, the more she wanted to swipe one of the cheesy Zippos in the display case behind her and set fire to the Irish Spring. The whole store. Everything. Engulf herself, this woman, and her unborn child in the flames.

Angie's relationship with Paul had begun with an English ivy plant. She was walking by his classroom one Tuesday after school when she noticed him misting its leaves with a spray bottle. She wasn't sure what made her stop, exactly. Maybe it was the way he gingerly touched and separated the leaves, careful to wet each one. Or the tender way he looked at the ivy, as though he were gazing into the eyes of someone he loved. It shocked Angie, her fleeting thought: *How lucky to be that plant. Those leaves.* And before she could gather her wits, Paul looked up, smiled his thoughtful smile, and invited her in. He asked her how she was getting on with *As I Lay Dying*, and they chatted for an hour, an exchange that made her feel as light-headed as the first time she inhaled nicotine.

A few days later, she'd stopped by his car after school to ask a question about the syllabus. He told her to hop in and they drove around talking and smoking. It was the most thrilling conversation of her whole life—they chatted about southern Gothic literature, the novels of Charles Dickens, punk music, the Iran-Contra scandal, the play Paul was writing. When he dropped her off at home, he had looked at her in such a way that she'd swear he'd reached across and caressed her face the same way he touched those ivy leaves. "Angie, you've got everything you need. Take the SATs and go to college," he said. "That's where you belong."

Angie stared at Joanna's belly, at the piece of Paul that was floating around in there. At times, she'd thought she'd wanted his baby, not right then but someday. She'd allowed herself to indulge in a fantasy of him divorcing his wife, moving to California with her, so Angie could attend Stanford. She'd go on to get her PhD in comparative literature, they'd raise a daughter who would know nothing about her Meyer roots, and he'd finish that play.

Joanna was beginning to fidget, smoothing her dress and fiddling with a cuticle. Why did Angie have such difficulty meeting her gaze? It wasn't like her to feel uncomfortable in the face of an adversary. In all the times Angie had daydreamed about this moment, never once did she have difficulty looking Paul's wife in the eye.

A few days after that first car ride, Angie had again waited for Paul after school. He drove her to the outskirts of town, to the lot he and his wife had recently bought, upon which stood a newly poured foundation. They sat in his car, talking for a while, sharing a cigarette. Then he reached over to put his hand on Angie's thigh, but recoiled before touching her. A long moment of silence passed as he stared out the window, his jaw twitching.

"I don't think I want to build a house here," he said, finally. "I don't want to build a house at all. But it doesn't matter, does it?"

"Maybe not," she said. It struck Angie how different their lives were. No one bothered to count on her, but people depended on Paul—his wife, his students. Yet here they both were sitting in a smoke-filled car, staring out into empty space that would soon be enclosed by walls, brick by brick. "Let's pretend that we don't live in this stupid town," Angie continued. "We're just passing through. And this house belongs to . . . strangers."

She reached over and grabbed Paul's hand, rubbed the back of it against her cheek, and that was all it took. He turned and kissed her urgently, his lips softer than she imagined. Paul was an attentive and confident lover, two qualities she'd found sorely lacking in boys her own age. Soon they began meeting after school a few times a week—driving out to that lot, talking, and then making love. Later, she'd realize that they never once used the backseat, that she always straddled Paul in the front—shielding him from the view of his future house.

"Is that man coming back with the soap soon?" Joanna asked. "My husband's waiting outside for me."

Angie whirled around and spotted that familiar blue Buick parked across the street. Her hand began to shake as her co-worker returned with the Irish Spring. There was Paul, sitting in his car, reading the newspaper, like nothing at all had happened, like Angie didn't have the means to ruin his life. Ruin all their lives.

"That'll be $15.32," Angie said curtly.

The day it all changed, she and Paul drove to the lot like they always did. His brick house, painted white with black shutters, was nearly finished. Leaning stiffly up against his car, Paul told her his wife was pregnant. That he couldn't do this anymore and that he was sorry. He had done wrong by Angie. By both of them. Angie had begged, pleaded—things she did not do. But he was immovable. Pain gathered deep within her belly, cascading outward until she could feel it flowing, viscous and toxic, through her veins. Angie had called him names and slapped him, and he'd done nothing but stand there, which only increased her fury. Then she opened her mouth and spewed her poison: *I'll tell her. I'll tell everyone what you did. How you fucked a student.* The hurt in his blue eyes nearly knocked her backward.

"Here you go," his wife said, handing Angie cash. "Are you sure you're all right? You look a little peaked."

Angie nodded and counted back the change, now returning Joanna's gaze. She had thought that she'd be able to coax Paul into changing his mind. But not only did he refuse to see her, he ignored her in class, barely making eye contact and writing little on her papers beyond the letter grade he assigned. She felt like Mr. Rochester's wife in *Jane Eyre*, locked in a room, slowly going mad. Alone.

The pain within her churned until it seemed that if she didn't do something it would spew out of her like oil shooting from a well. So one day, she cut Paul's class, took out her keys and made long, deep striations along both sides of that Buick. With a pocketknife, she punctured each of the tires, just as he had punctured her heart.

Angie hadn't counted on the janitor taking out the trash and catching her mid-jab. Paul had stood there mutely while the principal chastised her. Perhaps he was too nervous or too angry to comment. She would never know. Given her track record of suspensions, they had expelled her without a second thought.

"Thanks," Joanna said, gathering her shopping bags. "Hope you have a nice afternoon."

As she turned to leave, Angie's heart raced. Here was the moment she'd been waiting for, the opportunity to inflict as much pain as she had felt. The thought of it had gotten her through these intellectually barren days, the bleak prospect of her future. And really, didn't Joanna deserve to know what kind of man the father of her child was?

"Wait—your husband . . . ," Angie started.

"Excuse me?"

"Your husband, I know him," Angie said, clearing her throat.

"Oh, you do?" Joanna replied, crossing her arms in front of her chest. "How?"

Angie turned to look out the window again at Paul. He deserved this. Yet she couldn't get a phrase out of her head: *You know better*. Angie wanted to shout the truth in Joanna's face. She wanted to open her mouth and coat this woman in the roiling, obsidian muck that threatened to drown her from the inside every minute of every day. But she knew better.

As she looked at Joanna's befuddled expression, for the first time, Angie thought about what would happen after her revelation. Upon the gratifying release of the truth, after his wife had backed out of the store crying, Angie would still be working at DrugMart. Paul would still be out of her life. She'd still be expelled. Her SAT score would continue to mock her from her pocket. *But at least you wouldn't be alone in your misery*, a silken voice in her head insisted.

"How do you know him?" Joanna repeated, cocking her head to the side.

"I . . . I . . . uh . . . ," Angie stammered.

She couldn't shake the sensation that this moment marked the point where the river that had been carrying her along finally diverged. Down one channel was the Meyer girl who slept with her teacher, who got herself kicked out of school, who lived in Pocomoke for the rest of her crappy life working one dead-end job after another, who ruined a woman simply because she wanted someone else to be just as unhappy as her. Down the other channel was a girl named Angie who made a mistake, who repeated her senior year at some other school, who found a way to go to college, who left Pocomoke and never looked back.

"I . . . I got a 1450 on my SATs," Angie finally blurted.

"Oh, that's terrific," Joanna gushed. "You must be one of my husband's students."

"Yeah, I am—I mean I was," Angie said. "I graduated. Just making some money before I start school at Stanford."

Her lie was so delicious she could almost believe it. For the first time since Paul had dumped her, Angie felt like she could breathe. Yet knowing he was out there, across the street like that, ignoring her just like he had in class, stirred the pain inside Angie. It reminded her how pleasing it had been to hear the hissing of the air leaving his tires and the scraping of her blade along his car.

"Your parents must be so proud. Well, I have to run, but good luck," Joanna said, waggling her fingers goodbye.

"Thanks, and please tell Paul—Mr. Carter I mean—that Angie says hi."

TATTOO EMPORIUM

By: Kip Robinson Greenthal

My daughter Mattie calls me from downtown and says she needs my signature so that she can get a tattoo. She is sixteen, and she needs to be eighteen to get one. I am unhappy about this, but I get in the car anyway and drive to where she has asked me—the Tattoo Emporium. A mood, dense like coiled vapor inside my head, follows me as I drive through the dulled rainy air of city streets.

I recall years ago standing with a five-year-old Mattie and her father on the crest of a field, flying a kite the shape of a small red bird. The sky is cobalt over the ocean, which lies at the foot of the slope. We are laughing as the kite sweeps down toward us in the wind draft, and then darts back up into the blinding sun. The motion reminds me of a small hawk I'd seen learning to fly from the field's edge.

Then I remember driving a three-year-old Mattie in the snow to the hospital in the middle of the night when she had an asthma attack, and I try to recapture that simple power of loving, when parents do anything to protect their young. At points of danger when she was a child, I'd say to her: "Mattie, do what I ask because I'm asking you," and Mattie would always do it. We loved each other: spending afternoons curled up together reading fairy tales illustrated by Arthur Rackham, planting peas in the warm earth, or talking about kind people and why some people do cruel things. But in the past few months, I've been picking up Mattie at two in the morning because she's drunk too much beer, and I've found her retching on a friend's bathroom floor. I grip my hands on the steering wheel as I drive down Pike Avenue toward the Tattoo Emporium, and my stomach rolls like a steel drum.

Two months ago, I was washing dishes in the kitchen late at night. Mattie came up behind me, stood so close, her breath fire against the skin of my neck. "Please, I have something to tell you now," she said. I turned. My hands were still in the warm water. Mattie's face was tear streaked. She had left school that day, gone downtown, and had stolen underwear. Expensive bras, underpants, indigo and sea green lace, totaling $455. Security guards had picked Mattie up and called me.

"What do you want to tell me, Mattie?"

"Dad makes me . . . " She stopped, then choked. "Sleep with him."

My hands, still in the water, dripped out toward Mattie. But she backed away, staring at me, as if startled by her own words. The ceiling light blazed like a disc over our heads while "makes me sleep with him" clanged around the room.

Suddenly, my life became a single sense—sight. I had not seen this happen, so how could it be? My thoughts raced, a spring coil—the face of Mattie's father ricocheted in front of me. We divorced three years ago; one day a week Mattie stayed with her father. I wanted to pluck out my eyes. Falling against the sink, I tried to unsnarl the muscles in my voice so that I could speak.

"When, Mattie?"

She didn't like the question. Mattie looked at me sideways, her dark half-face.

"I'm not sure . . . ," she hedged.

My head felt compressed between slabs of ice.

"Mattie, tell me, when does he make you sleep with him?"

She stared down at her feet, ground them into the floor.

"I can't tell you exactly."

"Mattie, this is serious, I need to know."

"Just believe me, Mom." She sounded angry.

"Can we talk?"

"No. I just needed you to know."

Mattie ran from the room.

I remember the plate I was holding when she told me this, the pale blue glaze, the line of chocolate brown trim. Mattie's words fired into the plate and became its shape. I saw her face, the face I loved more than any other in the world, her eyes large, a whole of beauty unto itself. The air I breathed scraped inside my lungs.

That night I lay in the dark, my eyes wide open. They wouldn't close, the eyes that hadn't seen Mattie's father make her sleep with him. I loathed my eyes. Mattie's father looked at me from the ceiling, and his face rolled as though it were floating under a river. I saw all three of us flying kites again, and the image cracked in ten thousand pieces.

A red-scripted neon light burns a patch through the rain from the side of the street. Tattoo Emporium glows through the slit window of a storefront, and I am relieved to find this place. Mattie has given me good directions. I park my car, go to the front door, and walk in. The narrow room is yellow and old, posters hang from the wall with large exaggerated pictures of lions, naked women, kangaroos, and bears. There is the smell of crushed ink. Two men stare at me from behind a counter, muscles in their forearms blimped through their skin. They must lift weights. Ink snakes, leaves, and flames twist up their arms. Dressed in black leather vests and pants, hair oiled back, they look at me indifferently, then return to drawing tattoos on other people's arms behind the counter.

I stare at the blue ink lines flowing like blood from the needles in the men's hands. I hear a whirring whine sound, the staccato beats of the needle point creating circles, mermaids, and "Mom" in a heart. In their skin, I see an imaginary world and catch my breath.

A voice startles me. "Are you Mattie's mom?"

I turn to see a pale, thin girl who has come from a back room.

"Yes," I say, nodding at her.

Mattie emerges from the same room and looks at me with sweet, watery eyes. Standing a foot from the girl, her short blond hair waves a delicate pattern around her face.

"Thanks for coming, Mom," she says.

In my mind, I hear Mattie's screams. Earlier this same day, we'd yelled at each other. I'd told her she could dye her hair black, she could pierce her nose—those were things she could change. But once she got a tattoo, it would be permanent.

"That's just it," she yelled at me, slamming the door. "I want something that can't be changed."

And now I am with her in the Tattoo Emporium, with the pale girl, maybe five years older than Mattie.

"I need your driver's license along with your daughter's," she says with Mattie standing beside her. I pull my license out from my wallet and hand it to the girl, and she takes Mattie's too and puts them in the photocopier. Mattie and I are copied together—Mattie's face next to mine, our birthdates alongside—and the light fuses us into one, ignites our skin. I sign my name, scrawling my signature as if it's important.

"Mom, will you come in the back with me while I get my tattoo?" Mattie's tone has sweetness in it.

I'm startled by this gesture of intimacy after days of barely talking.

Sure," I say, slightly numb, scarcely knowing where I am, still seeing my face bound under the light with Mattie's. I follow her into the back room with the girl.

Mattie goes over to sit on the black leather bench. She pulls out a picture from her pants pocket that she hands to the girl. "I want this."

The girl studies the picture—a hawk etched on the shield of a Greek warrior—and holds it to the light. Her skin matches the pallor of the dirty yellow walls and the dirty brown rug beneath her. There is the scent of wet chemicals in the air. I sit in the chair beside Mattie, watching her stretch out on the black leather table, thinking to myself that I'm holding my daughter's hand while she is getting a tattoo.

"I only want the hawk," Mattie says.

"Not the shield?" asks the girl.

Mattie says no.

The girl walks to the back of the room with the picture and photocopies it. There is a whir and a slip of light like a flashlight in the forest. Coming back to stand beside Mattie, the girl holds up the hawk for us both to see, the fine-lined curve of its wings. This bird will fly through my daughter's skin. Mattie lies suppliant, and her long, stretched-out body makes me think of her father lying beside her. But I cannot see her body against his.

I cannot see this.

But I can see Mattie's father. I see him on a motorcycle, his legs strong, bowed out; he's ready for the road under a heavy sky. Mattie acts as if she expects nothing from him now.

"He'll tell you it's lies," she said.

I feel nervous in the Tattoo Emporium, and need to talk.

"How did you get into this business?" I ask the girl while she studies the hawk. I want her to think my sitting here holding my daughter's hand while getting a tattoo is normal, as if Mattie were a small child getting a polio shot.

The girl looks at me, eyes flat as buttons.

"It's limitless," she says, smiling, her skin suddenly brightening. "Drawing tattoos is limitless."

"Oh," I say. The walls of the room are floating in my mind. The girl takes another photocopy from the machine and comes back to the black leather stretcher on which my daughter lies. Reaching out, the girl's fingers touch my daughter's hip.

"Where do you want the bird?" she asks.

Mattie unfastens her belt and lowers her jeans.

"Here," she says, pointing to the small hollow where the upper thigh meets the pelvis. She tells the girl she wants the bird just beneath her pelvic bone. Her hip bone is like a small mountain curved in the blue air. I swallow hard. The girl pushes the image down to where my daughter's fingers lay.

"But the bird is flying away from you," the girl says quietly as she places the image on Mattie's skin. My daughter's eyes meet hers, then shift down along her body. She sees the fine-lined bird going away from her and looks confused.

"I can reverse the image," the girl says quickly. "So that it will fly toward you."

"Yes," Mattie says, looking at the girl. "I like the bird coming toward me." Her fingers move down to the hollow spot. "Put it there," she says.

The girl smiles. Turning the paper, she reverses the image, pushes the bird in on Mattie. Purple lines on tracing paper stare back, and the girl turns, gets the needle ready. The point vibrates, and the girl fills it with dark blue ink and pushes the needle down. It whirs in and out of Mattie's skin like tiny jets, fragments that shoot a trail of stars. The needle moves down through the flesh, and leaves an image of wings, an arched head with some blood, and Mattie's flesh shakes, loose and fragile. Holding my hand, Mattie closes her eyes. She takes in the pain of the sharp needle.

"I'm glad the bird's coming toward me," she says looking up at me. And the slow, emerging shape flies up through the soft folds of her, and reaches over her skin to light there, holding out its wings as if to dry in the fragrant air.

But that hawk flies right into me—rips open my heart. I sit watching my daughter. How could she have told me the truth any other way? The bird comes low over the pelvic bone, into the field of the dark triangle of her; it comes to stay there forever.

First published in *Currents: Favorite Selections from Shark Reef Magazine* in 2004.

EYES SHUT

By: Susan Bloch

"**W**ho on earth is that?" My father asked, banging his scotch down on the table.

He followed our "house boy" to the hall. It was the mid-1950s, and a loud knocking at the front door of our Johannesburg home in the late evening was unheard of, unless guests were expected.

Dad's tall frame towered over me as the door opened. He grabbed my hand and pulled me close to his side when three burly policemen stepped into the hall. I was five years old, and I remember clinging to his leg feeling that something bad was happening.

"We've inspected your servant's quarters," a stern man announced, thumping a baton on the palm of his hand.

His khaki uniform was crisply ironed, and I was tall enough to see his icy green eyes. I looked down and noticed the front of his brown shoes. They were so shiny that I could see my face staring back at me. My ringlets were shaking as my head trembled.

"We're jailing that girl." The policeman's stern voice filled the house, as he turned to look backward out the door.

A loud wail echoed in the driveway. Greta, my black nanny, was sobbing hysterically. She was being shoved into a cage at the back of a police van. Her apron covered her face. Was it shame or fear? Howls of despair filled my heart. Wails of Zulu anguish. My head began to hurt and my ears were ringing. I pulled away from my father and ran toward Greta.

"Oooh nooo you don't!" barked the policeman.

He grabbed my curls and jerked me back into the house.

Unaccustomed to physical abuse, I yelped, holding onto my head.

My mother, who'd been dressing for dinner, cowered in the passage and pulled me toward her with shaking hands.

"You stay with me and don't go running off," she yelled. "What do you think you're doing?"

I felt smothered by her familiar perfume—Chanel No. 5. I'd learned to read the label on the square glass bottle. It always made my nose tingle. I thought it was silly to have that disgusting smell on her. I stood still, afraid to disobey her, but was upset that she scolded me.

Right then, my nanny, whom I adored, was being taken away, and I didn't know why. Greta's large breasts were shaking under her arms, and instead of her normally contagious laughter, all I heard were horrifying shrieks. I wanted Greta to hold me and comfort me as she always did. I was too young to know she needed my help.

Earlier that day, I'd tried to help Greta with the laundry.

"Beee careful now," she'd chortled, hugging me with her large wobbly arms as we worked. "Let me hold the grater soooo you don't cut your fingers."

The lemon laundry soap dropped into the hot suds. While the machine was washing, we went into her room, where she showed me a photo of her standing next to a young boy.

"This is my kiiid, Alex. That's my auntie's house behind us," she added proudly. "She looks after him while I'm working here."

I wondered if she missed her son, but was too shy to ask.

"You know my village is very far away. It takes a whole, loooong day to get there by train. I go home only once a year to visit my family," she continued as if she'd read my thoughts.

Greta's room was meticulously tidy. Her bed was covered with a starched sheet she'd embroidered with red and green cross-stitch. Her uniforms were folded on a small shelf. Blue with white piping, blue caps, and white aprons. A navy dress hung on a wall hook. A cake of carbolic red soap lay on the windowsill.

"They smell worse than us," my mother had told me, when I asked why Greta's soap smelled so strong. "They need a pungent soap."

To me, Greta always smelled of fresh laundry. I didn't quite understand, but knew better than to ask too many questions. My mother always had an excuse for why Greta was different from us. But then so did my aunts and uncles, and my schoolteacher. I often remember hearing that "those people" smelled bad.

When I wanted to give her a sip of my milk, Greta would politely decline. She was well aware of black people's protocol.

My mother warned, "We give them different plates and cups so we won't get sick from them."

"Also they prefer their own food," Mother retorted, when I asked why they ate mostly bread and jam and *mielie pap*, porridge made from corn.

"You know what your problem is?" she'd continued. "You ask too many questions and that'll get you into trouble one day."

My mother often disapproved of my independent spirit and tomboy ways. Most of the time I listened to her, but that evening I was angry. How could my parents allow my Greta to be carted away? And why?

"She had a visitor in her room," barked the policeman. "And you all know that's not allowed. You must take a closer look at what your kaffirs are up to." His green eyes continued to glare at me.

I didn't understand why any of this was happening. I didn't know that the police regularly patrolled white neighborhoods, checking to see if their servants, who lived in the backyards, had any visitors. Not even children were allowed. Apartheid affected every corner of life.

"Go to your room," my father ordered me.

Usually, there was no disobeying him. But my fury refused to subside.

"Get Greta back, Dad," I yelled hysterically, as Mother jerked me away.

Greta did come back a few days later. I cried myself to sleep every night until she returned. When she did, I first saw her stooped over the stove. I ran to her as I looked for her smile. Instead, her sad eyes haunted me.

"Is Greta going to stay with us for good now?" I asked at dinner that night, unable to chew or even swallow her crispy roasted potatoes. "And, why is she so sad? Did they hit her?" I continued into the stubborn silence, broken only by my mother's knife clattering on her bone china plate.

My parents exchanged glances. "Why don't you just finish your dinner now? We'll talk about it later," Mother sighed.

We never did talk about it—ever. And I'm ashamed to say that, even as an adult, I never asked Greta about her traumatic experience. It was easier to protest the brutal death of a stranger—Steve Biko, the anti-apartheid activist, who died after being tortured in jail—than get too involved in the pain and plight of someone I loved.

Looking back now, I understand how important it was for many of my parents' generation to fit into the system and not rock the boat. If they had, they would've not only incurred the wrath of an extensive and close family network, but they also would have experienced harassment and perhaps internment at the hands of the police state. Some did fight apartheid's fascist rule, but very few. Outspoken journalists or political activists were silenced under house arrest or fled the country. The rest of us "armchair liberals" held whispered discussions about some of the bad things happening around us. At the same time, we enjoyed a luxurious lifestyle, only made possible from cheap, oppressed labor.

There were multiple instances of injustice that jarred my consciousness as a child. Separate beaches, separate train carriages, separate shop entrances, and black families torn apart by fascist rules. Even now, decades later, so many of my friends and family members claim not to have known the extent of pain the government policies were inflicting on non-whites. They were only kidding themselves. We all knew. The apartheid era highlighted the ordinariness of good and evil. I guess it's natural that people in that particular time and place encountered both, and went on with their lives, no matter what. Perhaps it suited us not to care. Or to avoid asking too many uncomfortable questions except in the safety of our homes.

When I was in high school, several events changed my world. In 1960, at a demonstration against the law requiring blacks to carry identifying passbooks, police killed sixty-nine unarmed black protesters in the township of Sharpeville, thirty miles south of Johannesburg. Then Nelson Mandela was tried for treason. The secret police kept tabs on demonstrators. Often they disappeared in the middle of the night never to be seen again. I realized then that I either had to work to change the system or leave the country, but I was frightened of going to jail, and I didn't want to endanger our family. After all, we were Jewish immigrants to this racially divided land. We knew our place amid the prejudices and social tensions. I began to understand that all that's needed for evil to succeed was for decent people to do nothing.

As my father often remarked, "If it wasn't for the blacks, coloreds, and Indians, they'd be after the Jews again."

After graduating from university in Cape Town, I applied for a job at the Race Relations Board, a nonprofit organization that researched the impact of the horrific inequalities of apartheid on the health and education of blacks. My father received another warning from the police, who'd been following me and recorded places I'd visited. That organization was considered a communist breeding ground.

"Maybe you should think about going overseas for a while, now that you have your degree, " Dad wrote in his weekly letter. "Don't waste the best years of your life in jail."

He'd always given me good advice. I was scared, and realized that, like him, I was not brave enough to spend time threatened or locked up. As I slipped the letter back in the envelope, I closed my eyes and took a deep breath. I remembered the aroma of my father's scotch in the evenings, and the tobacco smoke from his pipe whenever I sat on his knee as a young child. A special treat was when he took a cigar from a wooden box and slipped the paper ring onto my thumb. Then he'd let me click on the lighter as he puffed away, the tip bursting into flame. His soft, gray eyes would twinkle through the smoke.

My dad had always been fair and generous with our servants. He'd grown up in a small town where he'd intermingled freely with the predominantly black customers, who came to shop at his father's store. At a time when blacks were not allowed to own land outside the limits of territories known as *Bantustans*, he'd bought Abie, our "garden boy," a farm. My dad was also one of the few people I knew who spoke Zulu fluently. We'd enjoyed many controversial political debates, and I knew, like me, he was anti-apartheid and did what he could to respect blacks in his own quiet way. There were so many harsh rules regarding the strict separation of the races in every walk of life. Greta, like all other servants, suffered awful apartheid injustices, while we whites lived privileged lifestyles. That's when and why a shy, unadventurous young bride and her husband left the country to study in the United States, and then immigrated to Israel.

Although my mother never dropped her prejudices, even in the 1970s and 80s when the apartheid regime was at its worst, Greta became her confidante. When my brother left his wife for another woman, Mother cried on Greta's shoulder, sharing all the sordid details that she was too embarrassed to discuss even with her closest sisters. She loved Greta, and called her "my special darling." Toward the end of the forty years she spent working for my family, Greta was finally allowed to eat the same delectable roast beef and chicken dishes she lovingly prepared for her "Madam."

When my mother became seriously ill, I was living in London. I spoke to Greta every week when I called home to find out how they were doing.

My brother retired Greta to her *kraal*, a Zulu village in the Bantustan, near the end of my mother's suffering when a full-time nursing sister was installed in the apartment.

"There's not much for Greta to do anymore now," my brother replied, when I told him how sad it must be for Mom and Greta not to be able to stay together and keep each other company.

Living so far away, it was difficult for me to counter his decisions. But I stayed in touch with Greta.

"Tell Greta I'm coming!" I'd call Abie, now a close friend, who'd continued to work for our family, taking care of my father when he fell ill.

Somehow he'd let Greta know through the bush "telegraph" when I was going to visit my mother. It took a series of relayed messages sometimes days to reach her. Greta would find someone to drive her that long eight-hour journey from Natal to Johannesburg to see me. She'd stay with her daughter-in-law on a small mattress on the floor in a tiny servant's room. She was still not allowed to sleep in our apartment. Apartheid rules could not be bent.

The last time I saw Greta was in the early 1990s when she came for my mother's funeral. We hugged and cried and laughed together. Apartheid was by then officially declared dead, so for the first time in her life I was able to take her shopping for new clothes in a mall that had previously been for whites only. Most of her clothes had been hand-me-downs.

Since Greta was suffering from high blood pressure and shuffled rather than walked, I pushed her around in a wheelchair. Black sales clerks surrounded us in awe.

"Owww, Mama," they laughed, clapping their hands in joy. "So wooonderful your princess can take you shopping. You are a biiig queen now."

"Wave to your audience, Madam Makakule," I said, smiling.

Giggling, Greta tried on her new clothes in a fitting room and left with bags of sweaters, skirts, scarves, warm stockings, and fancy underwear, to keep her warm and beautiful. We ate a lunch of roasted chicken and baked potatoes in a restaurant, served by a waiter. All things she'd never done before. I knew she might feel awkward, and she did at first, but I wanted to spoil her.

"Greta, you are still the best cook in South Africa," I said, smiling at the way her eyes shone in her new regal outfit.

"Thank youuuu, thank youoooooo, my baby," she crooned in reply.

She took a mouthful of food and nodded in agreement.

"I'm always cooking for everyone else," she sighed. "You know, this iiis the first time I'm eating food that someone else haaas cooked for me."

All those decades ago, without even realizing it, I learned so much from Greta. I never once heard her complain about the prejudice and the injustices of those times. Rather, she showed me how to deal with tough situations with quiet strength and fortitude. She always hugged me a lot. I'm sure as a young girl, she'd dreamed of having her own family in Zululand, not spending her whole life, from the age of fourteen, living on her own with a white family. Her aunt raised her four sons, and she barely saw them.

In spite of that, Greta was completely devoted and loyal to our family. I was devastated when she passed away five years ago. Even now, when I close my eyes, I can hear her piercing cries, as she was dragged to jail on that long-ago grim evening.

Only recently, did I begin to understand what Greta had taught me. Decades of living in New York, Israel, London, Mumbai, and now Seattle have not always been easy. I've had to learn new languages, work extraordinarily hard, and I've missed familiar faces. But I gained courage and confidence and tasted so many new experiences. Most importantly, I learned to be independent, no matter how hard it was—and still is.

When my beloved husband passed away, I was steeped in grief for months and couldn't help feeling sorry for myself.

"What would Greta do?" I challenged myself when I was most in despair. "How would she behave?"

As I struggled to return to living a normal life, I began to realize that it was Greta who'd taught me to adapt, to keep cheerful when times were tough, and never to grumble. Not by criticizing me, but by loving me. She didn't tell me what to do, but showed me every day. She was an unequaled role model on how to behave. Greta was my bright light during those dark years, and her light continues to shine.

CALLING FORTH

By: Laura Foreman

Western North Carolina, 1840

Late one night, after everyone at Dark Level Farm slept, Gabriel stepped outside the slave cabin he shared with his wife, Oglatha. His footsteps were muffled by heavy rain as he walked to the nearby shed. A blanket's coarse wet wool raked Gabriel's naked shoulders. Though only in his thirties, his back was already bent from years of fieldwork. Nearby he heard sounds, cloaked in the shadows of wet leaves, of those beasts that were still wild, hunting, their hungry tongues licking sharpened teeth.

Gabriel passed a scarecrow he had staked out at the edge of the garden. The bleached white face, carved from a gourd, resembled a skull, fierce enough to ward off any crow. *White folks think gourds and old rags be scaring crows off their corn. But they busy keeping evil away,* Gabriel thought. *Haints always be trying to sneak in and steal a life cause they ain't got one of dey own.*

Similar figures dotted most farms scattered across the countryside but few, other than those enslaved, knew that the scarecrow's secret origin was African. It was clear neither Miz Suzannah, the woman who claimed Gabriel and Oglatha as her property, nor her husband, John, knew anything of this hidden practice. Across the South, a great variety of altars—bottle trees, rock cairns, and any number of icons— had been subversively woven into the fabric of farms and plantations. Each served as a clandestine appeal to the all-powerful Yoruba God, Obatálá—a prayerful request for a life of purity and peace. That elements of Christianity were woven into the fabric didn't sully the intent. Suzannah had made her expectations clear. Each Sunday the slaves were to sit in the back of the small community church and listen to stories of burning bushes that talked, seas that parted, and men who walked on water. Yes, the slaves nodded each week. They, too, had witnessed such things.

For Gabriel and his wife, the spirit world was big enough for it all. Like water, spirit was a gathering of streams, each searching for a welcoming bed. Ultimately, in the confluence, there would be no distinguishing one stream from another. This wasn't something the couple ever spoke of; it was just something they knew. Because they knew everything had a spirit, and was alive.

Gabriel entered the small tool shed behind the barn. Inside, the damp air hung close with the blood taste of iron. He drew in a deep lung-full and rubbed his short beard, already flecked with gray. His footprints quickly vanished into the fine silt of the dirt floor. Rising up before him was his shrine to Ogún, one of the faces of God. The altar had gone undetected by both John and Miz Suzannah because it appeared merely as a heap of scrap metal piled around a block of cordwood. The wood was embedded with a variety of seemingly random metal refuse.

Gabriel pulled a muddy metal shard from his pocket and wiped it clean. Earlier in the day, his shovel had clanged against the metal bone of an old spade, its long wooden arm broken and decaying into dirt. He understood the discovery meant Ogún had summoned him. Using a stone, Gabriel now sharpened the blade until a keen edge flashed in the light of his lantern. Placing the weapon on the altar, Gabriel's breath rattled as an anchored memory shook loose of its moorings.

Although he could not clearly see her features, he knew it was his mother's face that was emerging. His image of her was dim; sometimes it was only a scent—the smell of wood ash in a woman's clothes—that brought her back. Gabriel was only nine years old when he had been sold by her owner. Yet some part of his mother remained, tucked deeply into the folds of his memory. Now it was her voice, low and certain, which echoed.

"Gabriel, come here," she growled as she sat on a rock outside the small windowless building where they and eleven others had slept. "Now!"

Six-year-old Gabriel knew he was in big trouble but not why. Head down, he slunk over and stood in front of his mother. She reached up and, without warning, slapped him across the head. It wasn't the first time she had lashed out to punish her son, but this blow was, by far, more severe.

Gabriel reeled backwards, stunned. His face burned from the back of her hand and tears welled up in his eyes.

"You can't be looking a white woman in the eye," she shouted. "You hear me?"

Gabriel flinched at the screech of his mother's voice. It reminded him of the owls he'd heard screaming at night. In terror, he shivered as goose bumps raced up his spine. His mother glared at him, her eyes locked onto his. He was trapped.

"How many times you been told?" she continued.

Gabriel shrugged, choking back tears. He didn't know what to say. He didn't know what she was even talking about. His mother's body shook with an anger that terrified him.

"Miz Eunice say you been sassing her—say you looked her straight in the eye." She grabbed Gabriel by the arm and shook him hard. "You can't be doing that—not ever." Her narrowed eyes burned through him. His mother's strong fingers tightened like claws around his stick-skinny arm.

"You hear me?" She gave her son another strong shake, her grip tightening.

Gabriel nodded, though he still didn't recall his offense. His small body shuddered, but he said nothing.

"Don't give 'em a reason to sell you off! I got to keep you with me!" Again he heard her owl voice scream out.

Gabriel didn't know that just over in the next cabin, another woman's child had been taken that very morning. Taken while the child's mother worked in the fields. An eight-year-old boy, stolen from his mother and sold at auction to the highest bidder.

"Can't you see?" his mother pleaded. "You're my only boy." She reached for her son, but Gabriel took a step back. His mother began to cry, and he watched great drops of water course down her cheeks. "I can't let 'em sell you off. I just can't." His mother's head sank into her open palms.

But Gabriel was sold—placed on a scale, his price determined by his weight. Then, as part and parcel of Colonel Stonewaller's property, Gabriel and many others were listed, not by name, but counted as one of so many livestock. As Gabriel grew older, his mother's scoldings gave way to cruel punishments doled out by the overseer who worked for Colonel Stonewaller. An Indian fighter, Stonewaller had taken a Cherokee woman for a wife so as to hold title to her land. It was from them, Suzannah's grandparents, that she inherited Gabriel and Oglatha. But, no matter how many beatings Gabriel had endured, his spirit hadn't been destroyed. And now Ogún, the warrior spirit of his ancestors, had summoned him.

A strip of red cloth, tied to a hoe handle on the altar, fluttered. Oglatha had given him the red fabric, a small remnant from her mending. Slowly, Ogún came to life. Gabriel reached out and pulled the crimson cloth to his face. The fabric was warm, like the beating of a heart. He opened the small cloth bundle he had carried from his cabin. Tucked inside was a slab of fried fatback and a wedge of cornbread. A dark stain seeped across the red bandana. Gabriel stared at the greasy bruise as if it were blood from a wound. Lifting the food to his nose, he inhaled the sweet fragrance of the supper he was now offering to Ogún in sacrifice.

In a low voice, he began chanting: *"Oloju ekun,"* Ogún, the cold. *"Oloju ekun,"* Ogún, the hunter. *"Oloju ekun,"* Ogún, the one with the unblinking eyes of a leopard.

Gabriel stared at two pitted brass rounds he'd found and had hammered into the wood. They glowed like eyes aflame. Rocking and humming, he summoned the power and protection of this Yoruba warrior among warriors. In this way, Gabriel held fast and was not broken, even though he was forced to live his life enslaved.

Lifting a heavy stone amid the pile of apparent detritus, he exposed a deep hole. He reached his arm into the opening and pulled out the various metal pieces he had buried. Then Gabriel felt for the cinched bag that sat at the bottom. It was filled with every coin he had ever earned. When Gabriel and Oglatha had first arrived, John had told Gabriel he was not to call him Master. In the early days, John had even paid Gabriel for his labor. As Gabriel came to understand John's ambivalence toward slavery, he'd resolved to use it to find a way to buy freedom for his wife and himself.

John had told him he needed $500 for Oglatha's freedom, $1,000 for himself. Oglatha's freedom would come first. With the weight of the bag resting in the palm of his hand, he told himself, *She's halfway to freedom.* Then, in a low voice, he sang his map song to freedom.

> *Follow the drinking gourd, follow the drinking gourd,*
> *For the old man is awaiting for to take you to freedom.*

In the night sky, the big dipper—the drinking gourd—always pointed to the North Star. It would guide him to the river and then to freedom.

Follow the drinking gourd, follow the drinking gourd,
For the old man is awaiting for to take you to freedom.

Carefully, he returned his treasure to the hole and covered it with what appeared to be discarded metal shards. He sealed the hole with the heavy stone.

Next, he picked up a hammer. As heavy rain beat against the roof, he pounded the thick splinter of a broken nail into the wooden block of Ogún's body. The wood did not split; Ogún's barbed shield bristled in the night. With each strike of his hammer, Gabriel grew stronger. Whatever it took, Gabriel knew he would fight for freedom.

～⌒೨

The next morning, Gabriel, in bare feet, stepped out of his cabin into knee-deep muck. With each step, the fierce spirit kindled during the night dampened. He saw Tsani, the Cherokee man who also labored at the farm, standing on a rock, his moccasins muddied. Tsani faced east, his eyes closed. He was one of the few Indians who had not been captured during the 1838 government roundup and expulsion of the Cherokee people from their native land.

Gabriel frowned, unsure of this man, a recent addition to the farm. The hue of both men was similar. Gabriel's skin was the color of ripe chestnuts, while Tsani's evoked the color of a clay bank exposed by angry water. The two men had been told they were to work together to repair the pigpens. Slick mildew gnawed at the pigpen's shingled roof. Black water dripped off the eaves, each drop plunking heavily into the pigs' water trough.

Gabriel shook his head remembering the day Tsani, nearly starved, had reluctantly come out of hiding. It had taken a couple of weeks for Gabriel, speaking in the Cherokee man's native language, to convince Tsani it was safe to accept the food offered by Miz Suzannah. As a boy, Gabriel had a knack for the local dialect and, as a result, he had always been the one sent to barter with the Cherokee for fish and berries. During those times, Gabriel had only caught a glimpse of Tsani in passing. But that was before the removal of his people.

Tsani stepped off the rock, and the two men headed over to the pen. The hogs grunted as a sow pushed up against Tsani. He frowned and shoved the beast back toward the center of the pen. The sallow-eyed sow waddled over to the feeding trough, the sacs of her swollen teats dragging through the mud. Though it was still early, already the sun beat down, hot and heavy. In the stagnant damp air, a thick cloud of steam rose up from manure piles, freshened by rain. The men choked on the stench.

Tsani, the shorter of the two, turned to Gabriel. "These *a dv si qua*," he said, his voice filled with disgust as he aimed his shovel at one of the filthy animals.

Gabriel nodded and said, "Hogs not from around here. Invaded the place with de Soto—way back." Because Gabriel spoke to Tsani in Cherokee, it gave the men a place of shelter, a language no one else understood. "Hogs sure have invaded the place—just like white folks."

Tsani offered a wry smile. "They make the deer vanish," he sneered, waving his arm in an outward expanse. The sharp blade of his black hair sliced the air. "Nothing left."

Gabriel knew Tsani was talking about both hogs and white men as he looked out at the land. The rain had reduced the place to a smear of red clay. It looked as if a festering wound had opened. The field of recently harvested corn stood forlorn, with the stubble of stalks broken and bent. The crop had been disappointing; too many ears were puny, with kernels that were mealy and tough. Off on the ridge, lush green trees teased like the mirage of distant water.

A hen flapped her mud-soaked wings in a futile effort to gain purchase on a dry roost. Sweat seeped from Gabriel's every pore. Needles of salt stung his bare back. With each passing day Gabriel was supposed to teach Tsani how to farm—how to live as a foreigner in his native land. Yet, Gabriel's efforts to convert the Indian man were met with constant resistance. Soon it became clear that Tsani was a man whose life would abide neither calendars nor clocks. Time followed the cycles of moons, shadows cast by the sun, and the whims of rain and wind. It wasn't long before their roles were reversed and Gabriel quickly learned to watch Tsani for signs.

One day, without warning, Tsani stopped work and stared into a clear sky. "Storm coming," was all he said. Gabriel scanned the horizon—no dark clouds had gathered. But the two men set to rounding up the chickens and tucking them safely into their coop.

Soon everyone began to depend on the native man's senses. Often it meant the difference between a gathered or a ruined crop. Without realizing it, all at the farm had left their European ways behind.

Day after day, the two men worked side by side. Then one night, Tsani pointed to the moon. "*Galoni*, the fruit moon," he explained. "Time to gather."

Early the next morning, Gabriel stood at the edge of the cornfield, the invisible boundary he could not cross. Both men worked for a share of the harvested food, but, unlike Tsani, Gabriel could not leave the farm without a pass. To do so could mean capture. Bounty hunters were known to round up slaves who didn't have the necessary script and take them further south for resale to large landholders. Gabriel knew their cruelty first hand. Colonel Stonewaller had owned a large plantation, and Gabriel still bore the scars from the vicious lashings he had endured.

As Gabriel watched Tsani vanish into the forest, he angrily worked a strip of Ogún's red cloth tightly between his fingers. Watching Tsani slip freely between the trees only reminded Gabriel he was enslaved and, in that moment, envy crept up his spine like a green serpent. He felt betrayed by the Cherokee man.

When Tsani returned, carrying bundles of herbs for medicine, Gabriel avoided him. Toward the end of the day, when Tsani came into the barn to help Gabriel with the evening chores, Gabriel snarled, grabbed an empty bucket, and proceeded to pull angrily at the milk-heavy teats of the old swayback cow. Tsani kept his distance and said nothing as he brushed down the mule.

After a few days, Gabriel's anger receded, and once again the two men worked side by side. The rains had given way to weeks of drought. Tsani looked down and toed a shard of dried red clay. "Come next spring, I expect I'll need to teach them how to plant beans and squash. Plant during dark phase of *Anisguti*, the planting moon. Harvests will triple."

Gabriel imagined bushels of beans and squash. "A good harvest— wouldn't that be something?" he said.

Years ago, John had allowed Gabriel to sell some of the okra he had grown beside his cabin and keep the money for himself. But as times grew leaner, John declared the okra, too, had to be part of the crop they sold in order to pay taxes.

"White folks always hungry. They want what you got," Gabriel said with bitterness.

Tsani glanced in Gabriel's direction. "True enough. They take everything; then start talking about God. Heard it all my life. Guess you have, too."

Gabriel nodded. "The more I see, the more I think they don't know nothing." He squinted and looked at the cornfield; a few dry stalks remained. The scarecrow grinned back at him. *Hidden in plain view*, Gabriel thought.

He looked up at the sky. Black clouds gathered along the ridgeline. He could smell the sharp metal scent of lightening. Ogún was with him.

REVELATION

"The truth is rarely pure and never simple."

Oscar Wilde

A SHIFT IN VISION

By: Barbara Helen Berger

One of the most exciting things I learned in art school was how to see "negative space." A drawing professor introduced it to his beginning class by asking us to shift our habit of vision. For weeks, we had been drawing the contours of objects in a still life. He had not allowed us to even look down at the paper while our eyes traced along the shapes of the pitcher, the lemons, the pile of wooden blocks, and our soft lead pencils followed. Then one day, he rearranged the still life and said, "Now. Do not draw the objects at all. Draw the spaces between them. Only the spaces."

At first, I felt as clumsy as if the delicate dance between hand and eye had turned inside out. Yet it didn't take long to discover that empty spaces had their own rhythms, their own shapes and proportions, their own grace. At the end of class that day, I leaned back to look at my pencil lines and was shocked to find not only the spaces I'd been so intently drawing, but also the bottle, lemons, pitcher, and blocks. They were all there—though they hadn't been the point—as a result of drawing empty space.

I found this thrilling. A marvelous secret had revealed itself. I went around trying to see it everywhere, focusing on the emptiness between tables and chairs, between people, buildings, tree trunks, branches. The campus was still full of students and trees, but the world blossomed with a hidden richness. It had been there all along, only not known to me before, never consciously seen.

Of course working with negative space is a necessary skill for any artist; we can't leave the empty spaces out of the whole we perceive, or the whole we try to create. As a student, I would soon realize how this new awareness improved all my own drawing and painting, but even beyond that, it seemed related to everything. Negative space was essential to things being in relationship with everything else, essential to any breathing room, and to any motion through the world.

Two years later, a different kind of space opened up—a valley of discouragement and despair. I fell right in. There were so many other skills to develop in art school, harsh critiques to endure, artistic growing pains, confusion, and self-doubt. Other students, no older than I, stood before their huge paintings and seemed to know what they were doing. But nothing was going well in my own work. What was it all *for?* Wasn't there some larger meaning, some greater purpose to find, to reach for in art, something that no one seemed to be talking about? No matter how many late nights I spent perched on a stool gazing into a mess of colors on a canvas, it seemed that the technical skills of painting were not, in themselves, enough. Not nearly enough. I felt lost in a secret struggle, reaching for something far beyond my grasp.

Then one hot day, I climbed on a bus with my summer classmates, headed out on a field trip. Everyone seemed lit up by a day's vacation from the studios, but I slumped in my seat, watching barns and trees and stone fences slide by, dragging my own despondency along. We came to Williamstown, Massachusetts, and a small museum I hadn't heard of: the Sterling and Francine Clark Art Institute. With no idea what to expect, I stumbled out of the bus with the others and went inside.

Cool, quiet rooms absorbed our busload of voices. Each of us began the more silent wandering one does in a museum, some proceeding along a wall in sequence, moving from one work of art to the next, others surveying the room first for whatever caught their eyes. From across the shining floor in the first room, one painting seemed to pull me. I walked slowly toward it.

Piero della Francesca, Virgin and Child Enthroned with Four Angels, c.1460-70.

I felt a great stillness. The Madonna filled the painting like a mountain, and the baby perched on her knee, so pale in his nakedness against the midnight of her robe, seemed to float there. He was reaching for a single small rose his mother held out to him. Around them, four figures stood like columns, as if to guard a sacred center. The artist had given only glimpses of their wings.

I would have no memory of how long I stood there, held in the atmosphere of that image. Nothing moved but my own vision, following masses of color, lines of composition. I had learned that diagonals and curves have a power of seeming motion, so that what is still may seem to turn, dive, or even soar. But Piero della Francesca had used these powers with a masterful restraint. He led my eye along subtle paths to every part of the painting, along a sleeve or a fold of robe or a carved lintel seen in perspective in the background. He invited my eye to keep moving, but also to rest along the way, settle as long as I liked on a face, a hand, a small gem fastening the Madonna's robe. He had painted every detail with equal grace, no extravagance. I stepped closer, then backed away for a larger view of the whole, then close again. There was no chink anywhere in the pervading stillness. The painting was charged with a presence I felt as actively serene.

Fellow students were moving on to other rooms. I heard their footsteps, but didn't want to leave the Piero yet. So I stayed in that room, and was soon alone with the angel in red who stood in the right side of the painting, his face turned to look out at the viewer. The angel was pointing a finger as if to say, "Look. Look there. Look again."

My eye had no choice but to follow the invisible line from the angel's finger. It led me to the heart of the painting. There, silhouetted against the night of his mother's robe were the baby's hands reaching out for the rose. The center of the painting wasn't the flower itself, but those small reaching hands. I stepped closer. Now it wasn't the hands, or the rose, that commanded my attention. It was the negative space between them. As I let my vision shift, the space itself seemed so alive it began to vibrate.

I looked up at the Madonna's face. Her eyes were unwavering. With a majestic calm she gazed downward to where she held the flower—close enough to invite her baby to touch it, and just far enough away that he had to reach.

What precision! The artist had made an eternal moment of that distance. He had filled it with a tension I could both see and feel. He seemed to have calibrated everything in the painting for this one space, as deep and blue and full of mystery as the Madonna's robe.

When Piero della Francesca laid his brushes down and stepped back to view his finished painting—in *oil, possibly with some tempera on panel,* as the wall label said—he could not have imagined it would someday end up in a small museum in a place called Massachusetts. He died in 1492. His burial was recorded the very day Columbus set foot in the New World. By that time, Piero had accomplished many fine panel paintings and frescoes in Italy, where he was born and lived. But in his lifetime, he was known more as a mathematician than as a painter. He wrote treatises on arithmetic and solid geometry, as well as a clear and groundbreaking work on the laws of perspective. Leonardo da Vinci, among other artists of the Renaissance, studied that book closely, as it was written especially for the use of fellow painters.

Perhaps Piero's own passion for the elegance of mathematical truth is what gave his paintings the calm and aloof sense of abstraction that would later appeal to many of us in the twentieth and now twenty-first century. He could not possibly have known how different the world would become, or what other forms of art would evolve over those five hundred years and more. Or that a young art student would someday stand in front of his *Virgin and Child Enthroned with Four Angels*, gazing, rapt, finding hope in the small, empty space he had shaped with such precision and care.

What was it about that space? How was it so heartening to me that long-ago day in 1966, and so memorable, I still think of it now?

It wasn't only the space itself, but everything around it. One doesn't come without the other, they are inseparable—I had learned that much, at least. This painting had a presence, a presence imbued with mystery. And though the mystery seemed especially located in that space between the Virgin's hand, the flower, and the baby's reaching fingers, I felt it running through the entire painting.

Something unknown was shaped and carefully, even lovingly, held by things that were known. The carved marble pedestal, the columns holding up a ceiling, the bodily mass and details of the figures, all these evoked our known, material world. The flower seemed to also, though it was shown in such an understated way, a flower so plain and generalized, I could not be sure if Piero meant a pink rose, as I'd first thought, or a pink carnation.

Some have said it is a carnation and symbolizes the crucifixion. If so, that might explain a seeming reticence in the Virgin's gesture. What mother would *wish* for her baby to grab hold of such a destiny, or even the ordinary suffering inherent in any human life? In a subtle nuance of Christian iconography, Piero may have hoped to convey a prophetic awareness in that eternal moment, a kind of inner knowing.

Every time I shifted my vision to gaze again into that small negative space, I found it vibrating with tension. Mystery lived in the dark spaces between the baby's fingers and the Virgin's fingers and the flower. Did the

Virgin withhold this flower by intention, or was she simply suspended in the act of giving? It was impossible to tell. Both might be true at once. Her face gave me no answer to the question. Instead, she reassured me with her calm. Though she seemed so aloof at first, her expression showed me a new possibility: a serene wisdom fully present to all that is ambiguous, beyond our reach, ungraspable, unknown.

To me, a young art student longing to bloom, entranced by the painting and falling in love with its beauty, the flower still appeared more like a rose than a carnation. Both are emblems of pure, undying love. But it could have been any flower, anything desired, longed for—a desideratum I felt intensely within myself, but could not yet recognize or name.

I came away from the Clark museum that day deeply heartened. Across a distance of five hundred years, Piero's painting had offered me a timeless gift. From the small negative space he had made so alive, it began to dawn on me that the feeling of mystery itself, the presence of something never quite within our grasp, might be the purpose in art that I was yearning for.

A full breath of air filled my chest. I, too, was a child in the lap of some vast mother who knows that we grow by the stretch of our own desire, even if we are not sure what we're reaching for. My own un-knowing wasn't a weakness after all, not a symptom of something wrong, something to fix or to solve. It was part of a greater mystery, and four angels were still standing in witness. I came away feeling at peace with the ungraspable quality that lies behind things, around and through and between things. Any life of art or spirit would always mean reaching into that unknown space toward what I love, but can't quite touch or hold. In the beautifully measured stillness of his painting, Piero assured me the mystery will always be here, and from its depth, I, too, will bloom.

First published in *Parabola* magazine, "The Unknown," Fall 2012.

OUT OF THE ETHER

By: Lindsay Pyfer

Standing behind my ten-year-old, Jordan, I listened as the scoutmaster recited the familiar words of the ceremony marking the transition from Webelo to Boy Scout. There were so many familiar faces in the audience: my parents, my husband, our older boy, our friends from the troop. So far, no one seemed to have spotted me for the imposter I'd become.

I looked the same: blond pixie cut, chocolate brown jeans, black sweater, and sensible loafers. But standing there, I was acutely aware of how different I was from the woman they knew me to be: the classroom volunteer, the PTA fundraiser, the steady wife. It was a struggle to inhabit the world I used to share with these people. I wasn't the same person anymore, and it was a huge effort to pretend to be.

I gazed at my son, at the dark hair, cut close to his head, the short-sleeved, flag blue scout shirt, the neatly tied kerchief narrowing to a perfect point between his shoulder blades. I had a decision to make and I knew that—no matter what I decided—someone was going to get hurt, and it had better not be this boy or his brother.

All my life, I'd been careful to do things "the right way." As the eldest daughter of an eldest daughter, I'd grown up in a blended family with seven children. Duty and self-sacrifice had been drummed into me. In an artifact from my childhood titled *Family Participation*, written in pencil on a faded piece of notebook paper after some infraction at home, my eight-year-old self promised:

1. I will help mommy and daddy.
2. I will not run off.
3. I will not dance in the daisies.

Now, at forty-six, I'd never run off in search of my bliss, unlike my mother, who'd fled her marriage for her lover when I was four. Maybe that's why bliss had found me, threatening my childhood resolve.

It happened on a sunny spring afternoon, in a low, white office building with windows of green glass. It was nobody's idea of a holy place.

The new leaves on the tree outside my office window quivered in the breeze. Soft daylight illuminated the photo of my two young sons on my bulletin board, and the Gary Larson cartoon I'd tacked next to it: a chicken hesitating at the side of a country road pondering a sign that read "The Other Side—Do You Need a Reason?"

I was seated at my computer, typing a list of issues for an upcoming meeting with my co-worker, Jonah. I'd received several rude emails from him asking for a status on the technical articles I was editing for his team of software engineers, who were hopelessly behind schedule. After I complained, my manager had dropped by his office to give him feedback about his communication style and then ordered him to meet with me.

"Knock knock." Jonah announced his arrival at my door, his voice a little shaky.

"Come on in," I said, steeling myself for the showdown I was sure lay ahead. I swiveled to face him, gesturing in the direction of my guest chair.

Jonah wore jeans and a deep blue shirt decorated with a pattern of white hibiscus, and his long dark hair was combed back and tied high on the back of his head. He sat and casually draped a leg over one arm of the chair. I'd been on the receiving end of Jonah's emails but hadn't seen him for months. Now I observed him, appreciating, in spite of my annoyance, just how perfectly genetic material can be combined in human form. I was captivated by his smooth skin, his boyish smile, and the long arch of his neck. I remember thinking he couldn't be more than thirty, more than a decade younger than me.

In the midst of a discussion about improving the collaboration between our teams, the ordinary turned extraordinary. Suddenly, a frothy, effervescent cloud welled up around Jonah's face. Then the cloud condensed and turned brilliant white. Solid beams of light streamed from his eyes, meeting in a single shimmering ray. I stared, incredulous, as that ray of light traversed the room and hovered a foot in front of me.

I felt as if I were falling forward, toward the ray of light. I checked myself. I was still sitting upright, elbows on the arms of my chair, my back against the back of the chair. But some part of me had fallen toward the light. A second later, I saw a shape—faint, but with definite edges, about the size of my fist—emerge from my chest.

In that moment, something happened that I can't explain, even now. The protective shield I kept around my heart crumpled, and my heart opened wide. This all happened outside regular time, as if time bent, because when the vision had passed, Jonah and I were still talking about how to get our teams on the same page. As I sat there trying to grasp what had just happened, I heard myself say in a disembodied voice, "I think everything will be fine now."

Then I stood. I needed Jonah to leave so I could collect myself. He stood, too. He looked pleased, happy, *changed* somehow. I walked him to my office door and pulled it open. On his way out, he smiled at me. Then he was gone.

The rest of the day was a blur. I was still in the thrall of the otherworldly encounter. Walking home from the bus that afternoon, inhaling the heady scent of blooming cherry trees, all my senses were heightened. The daffodils in their beds seemed utterly alert. I thought of Jonah's dark eyes and wondered if I'd ever have the chance to tell him how beautiful they were.

After that, it seemed Jonah was with me all the time, everywhere I went. His name popped into my head the moment I opened my eyes in the morning, and the thought of him comforted me as I fell asleep at night. I was as happy as I'd ever been, just knowing he existed in the world.

For a brief, glorious time, I believed that since I'd been shown this connection, which felt like an exalted kind of love, things would fall into place and Jonah and I would be together on the everyday plane. Though I'd met him my first week on the job, I now had the overwhelming sense that we'd known each other before, in some other life.

I came to understand the word "longing" in a way I never had. Sitting at my desk each day, I felt a pull from the direction of Jonah's office. We often bumped into each other at odd times, in unexpected places, for no explicable reason.

One afternoon, as I approached the stairs near my office, I looked up and saw Jonah striding toward me, his hair tied back in a sassy ponytail. As he stepped into the doorway that separated us, his skin suddenly appeared very dark, almost dark blue, like an East Indian god. His hair—unbound now—flowed out behind him, as if he were walking into a headwind. We looked each other in the eye and, though we were maybe eight feet apart, a heat emanated from him that couldn't be measured in Fahrenheit or centigrade, a heat that left me fighting for breath. I kept walking, aware that *once again* I was in an altered state of consciousness—at work.

Each time this sort of thing happened—and it happened practically every time I was near Jonah—I could only witness what was unfolding, my mind struggling to catch up. To me, these encounters seemed spontaneous, as if a powerful force drew us together. Did he engineer them?

It felt much too dangerous to ask. I was a contract employee; Jonah was on staff. I was married, he was single, and the company had a strict policy about sexual harassment. Even if I *did* summon the courage, how would I bring it up without risking my professional credibility?

I never had the chance to talk with Jonah about what happened between us. I have no piece of paper with a declaration of love, no email saved on a server somewhere, no token that would constitute physical evidence of his feeling for me. I only have what I witnessed: the ray of white light that extended from him to me, his happy smile, his laugh as a big silent ball of energy bounded between us when we walked together to a meeting, the way his friends looked at me, the way his girlfriend's eyes grew round when she spotted me a year and a half later, before she turned and ran.

Meanwhile, around me, life went on as it had before. In the evenings, I attended PTA meetings and helped my boys with their homework. At work, email was sent and received, editing was assigned and completed. Meetings took place. I spent my days trying to figure out who Jonah was to me, and what I could possibly do about it.

As a girl, I'd always had the sense that magic awaited me in the form of a special love. When my high-school English teacher asked our class, "If you could have one thing, what would it be?", one sixteen-year-old classmate, a swimmer, said she'd like to compete in the Olympics. Another student said, "To become a surgeon." My reply: "To find someone I really love who really loves me."

When the light passed between Jonah and me thirty years later, I knew my wish had been heard. But the granter of wishes had gotten the timing all wrong. I'd asked for a mutual loving relationship. Instead, my marriage had been threatened by a love that came from out of the ether.

My husband, Greg, and I had been together for nearly a quarter century. After some rocky times early on, I'd come to view our relationship as my greatest investment. Greg was my lover, the father of my children, the man for whom I'd promised to forsake all others.

I believed ours was a happy and enduring marriage and couldn't have imagined the way a few brief moments at work would test my commitment. All these years, my heart had had room for just one man. Now, somehow, I loved two. I'd always trusted myself—believed I knew what the right thing was—but nothing in my life had prepared me to cope with such divided loyalties.

It hurt me that some of my oldest friends—women who'd known me twenty-five years—didn't believe me when I told them about Jonah and the white light that had crossed between us. They rolled their eyes when I brought it up or changed the subject. It was clear that, in my friends' minds, I'd joined the ranks of marginal people, like the folks who claim to have been abducted by aliens. When I persisted, they urged me to get professional help. But from whom?

A psychiatrist was definitely out. I was afraid to call a psychologist. Would a therapist say I needed medication? Should be locked up? I had to work, to support my family. I couldn't falter.

Yet I was woefully unprepared for the mystical doorway that had opened in my life. Overwhelmed, I wept off and on, day and night: in the shower, huddled at the back of the bus on the way to work, in meetings, and quietly, on the living room couch in the middle of the night so I wouldn't wake Greg.

I wept because I was haunted by the sense that there's a higher level than this everyday one, present all the time, where nothing is random and every action has consequences. I wept because, though I knew my love for Jonah was profound, I also knew that if I even *touched his hand*, my marriage would explode and my children would be damaged.

So I wrote Jonah a note, crafting it carefully, aware that it might be my only chance to tell him how I felt. I acknowledged the attraction, and how special he was: smart, fiery yet gentle, wonderful to look at. I told him I wouldn't be able to forgive myself if I hurt my family. My hand trembled too violently for a proper signature, so I printed my name, fumbled the note into an envelope, and left it on his desk early one morning.

I'd done the right thing—I'd been honest about my feelings and had also protected my family. But once I truly understood that I might never have the chance to know Jonah in this lifetime—that a glimpse was all I'd been allowed—I was inconsolable. I had the overwhelming urge to hunker down in the lobby at work and emit a howl of absolute despair, like the bag lady I saw in Manhattan on a summer day as hot and wet as a steam room. In a fur coat and hat, her bags arrayed around her in the circular driveway outside a midtown office building, she had crouched wailing as well-heeled office workers strolled by, ignoring her pain.

Witnessing this, I'd been embarrassed for her, believing her to be mentally ill. Now I wondered whether she'd experienced something so painful, so incomprehensible, that she'd finally snapped.

The white light was no coincidence. I didn't make it happen, and I was pretty sure Jonah hadn't, either. I had the uncanny sense that it came from a different place, had been scripted. But why would God/Fate/the Universe—whoever— lob a depth charge into my carefully lived life, shattering it into a thousand pieces? Hugging the pieces to me, I tried to put them back together, but they didn't fit the same way anymore.

In an attempt to make sense of the senseless, I consulted rune readers, tarot readers, and psychics. Each had her own take on the situation. Some were helpful; others just made me angry.

After I caught a virus that was going around, my hips became so stiff and painful that I started avoiding stairs. I consulted an energy healer, Shana. As she worked, she asked what I was feeling and, lying there on her treatment table, tears streaming down my face, I told her about Jonah.

Shana told me she'd studied for seven years with a spiritual teacher, Mother Mildred Hamilton. "Each of us, during our spiritual evolution," she quoted Mother Hamilton, "is confronted more than once with extreme temptation. We have to meet that temptation from a higher part of ourself. If we succeed and resist, then we will bleed. But later, many blessings will come to us."

Shana had shared her teacher's wisdom to comfort me. But I wasn't comforted. Until then, I believed a mistake had been made, that someone in charge had miscalculated. But if Mother Hamilton was right, there was no mistake. Jonah was meant to appear in my life. I was meant to love him, and let it go. That's when I began to understand that my fondest wish—the connection I'd treasured—had been a spiritual test.

I felt like an actor in a play I hadn't signed up for. I hadn't been on a spiritual path. I didn't pray or chant, read sacred texts, or attend services. I had my hands full being a mother to my sons and holding my own at the software company.

Now I straddled two worlds, one foot in the realm of the five senses and the other in uncharted territory. I knew I couldn't live life in the old way. What I didn't know was what to do with the love and heightened awareness that had burst into my life with the ray of white light. Could I keep it? Must I turn it away, like Jonah?

I began searching for clues. The journey took me to inner places I hadn't known existed, some of them very dark. I had the overwhelming sensation that I'd been placed in a prison of the spirit with tall impenetrable walls, a bare earthen floor, and a roof that obscured all but a glimpse of sky. From time to time, a leaf would waft in or a small bird would alight on the wall, signs that life continued in full swing outside. I was stuck inside, alone, with no idea what I'd done to make this necessary, unsure if I'd ever get out.

Later, I read about the tight, uncomfortable places that characterize the dark night of the soul described by saints and mystics. But right then, it took everything I had just to hold myself together and start, little by little, to make sense of the spiritual path I'd been thrust onto. I wasn't always sure it was worth the effort. Still, I forged ahead.

Jonah married and left the company. We never spoke about what happened between us. Greg and I worked with a therapist to strengthen our marriage, to shore up the gaps in its foundation. Our sons grew into young men, in a home with two parents who loved them.

Then, one day, it occurred to me that maybe there was no need to prove anything to anyone—no need to solve the mystery. All that is required is a willingness: to accept it, coexist with it, and see where it takes me.

ALONE, NOT LONELY

By: Mary Anne Mercer

I was only a few months into my new life in rural Nepal when I realized that I was changing into someone I didn't really know. It had sounded like my dream job: two years working as a nurse trekking village to village in an exotic foreign land, leading a health team in a district with no roads, no electricity, and only one radio-telephone high on a hill. I was anxious to live a totally different life and learn about another culture, but I had no idea how much this adventure would teach me about myself.

My job was to go out for two or three weeks at a time with a team of Nepali staff who served as vaccinators and porters to conduct an immunization campaign and provide simple health teaching. One morning before starting the day's work, I decided to take a Nepali bath at the local water source instead of the usual sponge bath in my tent. I rose early, without the tea I was usually served before breakfast, and found Sita, one of the local women on my team, who said she would join me. We filed along a narrow path out of the camp and after a short distance came to a clearing.

Ahead of us, icy spring water poured out of an eight-inch square opening in a rocky bank covered with vines and vegetation, protected from view by surrounding bushes. The air was fresh, free of the dusty barnyard smells of the villages. Sunlight sparkled through the trees— enough for warmth, but without the unpleasant feeling that I was in a spotlight. *Here it is*, I thought, *my fantasy of living well with only simple, bare necessities without the trappings of civilization.* The spot felt peaceful, secluded. After weeks of feeling overwhelmed by crowds of people and constant activity, I was elated.

It was the perfect place to practice the public bath ritual that all Nepali women master, and two local women at the tap were happy to share their expertise. Wrapping a lungi under my arms and around my body, I worked my way out of the clothing underneath it, splashed icy water on the exposed parts, and then washed myself discreetly. With every chilling splash on my bare arms, neck, and legs, I could feel the tension lifting, my spirits rising. My flip-flops made sloshing noises on the rocky floor, and birdsong filtered down from the trees. I had learned that putting clothes on again over wet skin under the sarong was a challenge, particularly dealing with zippers. But it was worth it—the joy of feeling cool and clean, at least until the next hot afternoon of trudging up and down the trails.

I had nearly completed washing when I heard childish tittering from the rocks above us. I looked up and peeking through the bushes was a gaggle of kids ranging from about six to ten years old, delighted with their front-row view of this fascinating curiosity—me. They shrieked in delight when they noticed I saw them, preparing to flee and clearly savoring the excitement. These were the children I'd loved to tease and interact with when I first came to Nepal. But now, every muscle in my body tensed.

"Jesus! Sita!" I yelled. But then I lowered my voice. "Those kids are following me again. Will you get them out of here?" The momentary sense of peace was gone. *My blood pressure must be sky high*, I thought. *Why in the hell can't I get even a moment to myself?* That dull ache at the base of my rib cage was back in a flash, that feeling that I would never again be able to enjoy a relaxed, deep breath and the peace it brought. I couldn't believe how angry I was. *This isn't like me*, I thought. And once again I asked myself how long I would be able to do this work, live like this.

Sita whirled and gave her best schoolteacher admonitions to the group. "Kids! What are you doing here? You should be home helping your mothers!" They giggled some more then, seeing her serious expression, reluctantly drifted back out of sight.

With a scowl, I threw my washcloth into my bag and stalked back to camp. For the rest of the day, a porter was always on the alert, running interference with anyone who wanted to talk to me. He was polite but clear: "Come tomorrow morning if you need medicine—we will take care of you then. No, you can't see Memsaab now." Everyone seemed to be walking on tiptoes, hoping not to upset me.

That night a group of local young people were gathering with our porters in an impromptu session of local music and socializing. But I begged off and retired early, pleading exhaustion from the long day. I could enjoy the relative luxury of private "camping" within the four walls of the local school instead of the steamy confines of a tent, as classes were not in session. I blew out my lantern and settled into my sleeping bag, with the singing and laughter in the background a kind of comforting lullaby.

But a small horde of kids decided that the stranger camped inside the schoolhouse was more interesting than the music, even though there was nothing for them to see through the open, paneless schoolroom windows. After calling out a few times, they started throwing stones onto the corrugated metal roof, then giggling wildly, hoping for a response.

I'm just going to ignore them, I strategized. *They'll get tired of it pretty soon.*

The noise of each rock was shattering, like an electric shock, but I lay motionless in the dark. *I can deal with this*, I thought. *They're just having fun.* I'd always enjoyed the playful spirit of children that seemed to prevail in Nepal, no matter how constrained their circumstances or how few "things" they had. Eventually the noise stopped, and I dropped off into a light slumber.

Suddenly, I was startled awake by a small object landing on my chest with a thump. My heart pounding, I shrieked, not sure what was happening in the near-total darkness.

I sat upright, switched on my flashlight, and found the small round rock that had been tossed in by one of the children and had bounced off my chest. I could hear suppressed giggles coming from the open windows. Now, I was fully awake and very angry. *I'm going to kill those kids, every single one*, I muttered to myself. With that I bounded out of my sleeping bag and strode to the door, aware that the scrubs I wore for pajamas might look odd but were at least decent.

I threw open the door and could see a small crowd of kids, their grinning little faces full of excitement, lurking along the windowed side of the building. Grabbing the first boy I could see by his grubby collar, I charged with him into the middle of the crowd gathered around a fire on the other side of the building. Dozens of eyes turned on me, and the music and chattering abruptly stopped, bringing an uneasy silence.

I broke into a rant in my worse-than-usual Nepali. "These kids are throwing rocks at me! What can I do? I have to sleep—you need to stop them, right now!" Immediately, everyone was apologizing, scolding the children, and promising me it wouldn't happen again. Dil Man, one of our young porters, emerged from the group.

"Memsaab, okay, you can go back, we'll make sure they don't bother you anymore," he assured me. But the faintly horrified look on his face told me

I had overstepped the bounds of "annoyed" into something Nepalis were uncomfortable with—an open display of anger.

I shook my head in disgust, sighed deeply, and returned to the dark schoolroom. Already I could feel my temper slinking off like a chastised puppy, and an oh-no-maybe-I-shouldn't-have-done-that feeling rising in my chest.

Damn, I thought to myself. *I shouldn't have gotten so mad, but how much longer can I take this? What's wrong with me?*

Knowing that sleep would be slow to return, I sighed and crawled back into my sleeping bag. Losing one's temper is not a good thing in most cultures but particularly so in this part of South Asia. Maintaining balance, the appearance that all is well within the community, is an important principle of daily interactions.

Five minutes later, the music resumed, but more softly. *No more harassment from the kids anyway*, I thought. The singing continued into the night. I turned, sleepless, from one side to the other, wishing my thin foam pad were a real mattress. *What on earth is happening to me, the "nice" me? I* wondered. *Where is that kind, caring lover of children I'd been when I arrived?* This life was more frustrating, exhausting, and crazy-making than I could have imagined. I had never seen that angry, quick-tempered side of myself before. It felt like a mental illness, a total breakdown of the normal person I thought I was, as if some wicked alter ego was taking over. I was at once embarrassed and unable to stop my nasty reactions to regular, daily stresses. And when I thought of going on like this for days, weeks, months into the future, I felt my lungs collapse. There was only a dark, heavy space in my chest that wouldn't admit air, wouldn't open to the world.

I lay awake, going over and over the events of the day and the past few weeks. After only four months of fieldwork, I was emotionally exhausted. Being under continuous surveillance was something I hadn't expected, and I'd had no idea how badly I would react. I snarled at the first sign of being approached by anyone for *aushadi*, medicine, and frowned furiously at curious children observing my every move. The kids had been especially persistent, following me wherever I went and giggling at anything I did or said. I knew it was mostly because they had never seen a *bideshi*, an outsider, before, especially one with pale skin and blue eyes. But I felt like a hunted animal, and retreating to my tent wasn't an option. The heat required opening the flaps, and a mass of smiling children and curious adults would inevitably gather to stare at me, commenting on my every move.

With all the other stresses of life in Nepal, I was puzzled that the lack of privacy was the most upsetting. Not the heat, nor the exhaustion from hours of trekking up and down the hills every day. Not the flies, the fleas, the dirt, or eating the same food for every meal. It wasn't even the loneliness, as hard as that was. It was never having a moment to myself that was killing me—never being able to retreat from the world, to go into that private place inside me.

I had known about culture shock, and my brief orientation before leaving for Nepal included a rather vague explanation of the adjustments I would face with new food, the warm climate, and an unfamiliar language. But this was a different kind of stress, something more personal. I couldn't even explain it in Nepali since *iklaai*, the Nepali term for "alone," was also the word used for "lonely," with the subtle meaning that if someone was alone she was naturally also feeling lonely.

Still pondering what my behavior was telling me, what I could do about it, I eventually slipped into a restless sleep. The next day, I thought guiltily about the previous night, trying again to analyze the sources of my discomfiture. Certainly the work was more challenging than I'd expected. My main job wasn't meant to include providing clinical care, but I couldn't refuse to talk to the ailing or injured people who came to our camp. The small local clinics that should have provided care for the most common problems were often closed, and, if open, were frequently out of the most basic medicines and supplies. There were frustrating limitations to what I could do, although often a fairly simple remedy was all that was needed, such as recommending hot compresses for a wound infection. From the moment we started out on a trek until we got back to our field base, there were always eyes on me, people telling me their symptoms, asking for help and medicine, waiting for a response.

The very novelty of a stranger in the village might warrant a surreptitious trip to our camp in the hope of sighting the foreigner. The only time I wasn't aware of eyes following me was when I discreetly went off into the trees to relieve myself. They all understood what that meant—so only then would they grant me privacy. Otherwise, I was the hottest show in town. I was reminded of the cry of the reclusive Greta Garbo, the famous Swedish movie star of the 1930s, "I vant to be alone." Now I was she, a celebrity hounded by the public, and it was the worst fate I could imagine.

The other nurse in the program, who led a separate team, was excited about every aspect of this life, exulting about how amazing it was. Why couldn't I just "be here now," as the gurus instruct, in this fascinating once-in-a-lifetime experience? How could I even admit to being such a dull, limited character? It was a guilty secret I could only acknowledge to myself. I was too ashamed to even talk about it, to write about it in my letters home. The feeling that I was failing to fully appreciate this amazing opportunity was a secret burden lodged deep in my chest, and thinking about it made me close my eyes and take a deep breath. I wanted to exhale it out of my life.

Those first months in Nepal were devastatingly painful for me. I discovered a side of myself that I didn't like. Confusing things, unsettling things. It was as if I had met someone I didn't know, and only much later did I look back and find I liked her again. However, over time I was able to adapt by making full use of the quiet time that was available at the house in our field base, on trips to Kathmandu, sometimes even in my tent. All I needed was a room to myself, time to reflect, to write in my journal, and I felt renewed. But the pain of those early days stayed with me, a kind of blot on my recollection of my time in the field.

For many years, I was at a loss to understand why my equilibrium had been so disturbed during those first months in Nepal. Then years later, in a workplace seminar, I heard a lecture about the importance of personality types in determining an individual's reactions to life events. I listened to the speaker describe introverts as people who may be social and have fine interpersonal skills, but need regular time alone, quiet and unstimulated, to energize them, to recharge their batteries. When they don't have that, they feel anxious and off-balance.

I was suddenly alert. That's me! I thought back to my childhood in a family of seven children, remembering the times I'd pull away from my siblings to find a quiet place. The need for "alone places" became acute when I was an adolescent. I'd sit against the weed-carpeted side of my grandfather's weathered ranch house, next door to ours, and contemplate the horses in the pasture, the neighbor's small house and windmill half a mile away, and the badlands beyond. I dreamed about other worlds, places where I would someday go and the exciting life I would lead. When the Montana winter set in, rather than brave the chilly outdoors, I'd escape by curling up on the sofa and feigning sleep, with a blanket pulled over my head. Even then, needing my space.

As I recognized in myself the classic picture of an introvert, those early days in Nepal came back. Vivid memories emerged of the unrelenting attention of those endless crowds, and the bliss that encompassed me when I could finally go into a room and close a door on the rest of the world. It had been a perfect setup for making someone like me half crazy. Cut her off from the possibility of that interior, alone time; make her the undivided center of attention; surround her with an unfamiliar culture that values constant social interaction. No wonder those first months were so difficult. I gradually came to the understanding that that painful time was, for me, a normal reaction to being thrust into a totally new environment and culture combined with the assault on my introverted nature.

But those months in the villages of Nepal, immersed in the daily life of its people—their beauty and their pain—had many lasting benefits. My team became my family, bringing all the complexities and joys of family life. Challenging as it was, that time convinced me that work with people in other cultures was what I wanted to do. Since then, it has taken me to several continents where I have seen more of other places and other ways of life than I ever imagined possible.

Over the years, I've found ways to appreciate and nurture my need for space, for alone time. Although I treasure being with family and friends, time spent in my own company often provides my most creative and centered moments. What I learned from Nepal is something I cherish now, not as a guilty secret, but as a gift that allows me to embrace who I am.

MAY THEY BE HAPPY

By: Ursula Popp

I sat on rocky ground as I pulled my medicine bag filled with acupuncture needles and Chinese herbs from my day pack. Pale and limp, a young Tibetan pilgrim lay next to me. His pants and sweater were dirty, and he wore a warm woolen hat. The pilgrim was barely able to lift his eyelids to look at me. Wondering what was wrong, I gazed down at him.

"This man hasn't eaten for the past three days," Tempa, a young Tibetan monk, translated, "and has been unable to move for the past twenty-four hours. He suffers from severe stomach pain and cramps. It has taken him two months to get here. All he wants is to finish this pilgrimage. Could you help him?"

"I'll try," I responded, reaching for my patient's radial pulse, an important diagnostic tool in acupuncture. It felt empty. His pale, flabby tongue confirmed my diagnosis: exhaustion and lack of stomach Qi, a term used to describe illness in East Asian medicine. Gently, I lifted his sweater and shirt to insert a few needles in his abdomen, and then rolled up his pants to find the acupuncture points along his legs that would help his energy return. I filled a small plastic bag with remedial herbs for him to take over the next few days. As the needles did their healing work, I laid my hand on his shoulder for comfort and to give him some of my energy, of which I had plenty, despite the altitude of the Tibetan plateau, over 14,000 feet.

It was 2000, and I was on a pilgrimage to Mount Kailash with a group of twenty Westerners and an equal number of Nepali and Tibetan guides, cooks, and helpers. I'd chosen to undertake such a physically and emotionally difficult pilgrimage to one of the most remote places on earth as a prayer for a happier and more fulfilled life for myself and for more peace in the world.

Sitting with this pilgrim gave me a moment to appreciate the incredible setting. On my right, snowcapped Mount Kailash, the holiest of mountains for four major religions of Asia, towered over us. The mountain is sacred to Buddhists, Hindus, Jains and the Bön people, who practice a religion even older than Buddhism. In a perfectly pyramidal shape, Mount Kailash rose magnificently up from the barren, wind-swept Tibetan plateau to a height of almost 22,000 feet. Nobody has ever climbed this mountain except for the famous Tibetan monk Milarepa, who, according to the myth, went to its top on the first ray of sunlight early one morning.

It's believed that to circumvent Mount Kailash erases the collected bad karma of a lifetime. Though I had moved away from my strict Catholic upbringing in rule-driven Switzerland, with the fair share of guilt that comes with such a background, the thought of ridding myself of all the so-called sins I had committed in my life sounded very appealing. We had started our circumambulation that morning, after trekking over the Himalayan range through Nepal into Tibet for the past fifteen days.

Almost fifty years old, I had just completed my degree in acupuncture and herbal medicine, the education for which I had moved to the United States. Unclear if I wanted to return to Switzerland or stay in the States, I was generally unhappy and a low-grade aggravation permeated my days.

For years, I had been dreaming of traveling to Mount Kailash. It is one of the most remote places on this planet, very difficult to get to, no matter which way one travels. I was thrilled at the opportunity to make a pilgrimage there with a Buddhist teacher, and ready to offer myself up on this arduous trek for a more peaceful inner life. I hoped that travelling to a less materially saturated part of the world would give me direction and clarity. By offering medicine, I was grateful to be able to also bring something to the people whose homeland I'd travel through.

Returning my focus to my patient, I saw it was time to pull the needles. The man looked up at me with a big smile and a sparkle in his eyes. He was able to sit up and putting his palms together, he bowed in gratitude. I handed him the herbs, and Tempa translated the directions for taking them.

"I am so glad you worked with this man. Hopefully, now he'll be able to finish his pilgrimage," said Tempa, the short and delicately built monk who traveled with us and was my translator when needed. "Thank you."

"Oh, it was nothing," I replied dismissively and shrugged my shoulders. "I'm not even sure that what I did will help him in the long run."

"Please," the monk replied with urgency in his voice. "Do not diminish your work! It is your effort that counts. This man had been in pain, unable to continue on his pilgrimage for three days. Not expecting anybody to help him, he's immensely grateful to you and will pray for you for the rest of his life. This is how it is in our culture."

Tempa's words hit me hard, and I felt deeply ashamed. My cheeks flushed, my breath became shallow as I recognized the false modesty that my casual comment had revealed. My Swiss Catholic upbringing had taught me never to be prideful. "No need to boast," the nuns at school would say when I showed excitement about a project. Was my dismissal of my work one of the reasons why it never quite satisfied me? If I had the good fortune to be woven into this Tibetan culture where a person would pray for me for the rest of his life, I wanted to be worthy of such a prayer by appreciating the gifts that I was able to share. Humbled as I was, there was a quickening in my blood of excitement for a life in which I'd find joy and satisfaction in small gestures.

A couple of days later, we were to cross Dolma La, the pass that is over 18,000 feet high, the most sacred place on our journey, the culmination of our pilgrimage. We rose hours before sunrise to begin the arduous climb up to the pass. The American Buddhist teacher who had organized the trip had given us a most unlikely mantra for a pilgrimage, "Nowhere to go, nothing to do." Here it was again, the invitation for simplicity, helping me to find a rhythm of walking and resting.

At that elevation, the air is so thin that it was hard for my body to get enough oxygen. Putting one foot in front of the other, resting after every few steps, I moved slower and slower as I climbed the pass.

As I struggled, Asian pilgrims flew by me with smiling faces. Some of them made this arduous trek of thirty-two miles and an elevation gain and loss of 3,300 feet in only one day, while we took five. It must be a spiritual elation unavailable to me that carries them, I concluded. Then there were the pilgrims, equally dedicated, that I passed by who prostrated around the whole mountain—an inconceivable hardship. With pads on their knees and hands, they prostrated to a full body length. Then they'd put their feet where their hands had been to prostrate again, in this way mapping the whole trail with their body. What dedication!

Along the trail up the pass, thousands of shoes left by Asian pilgrims were piled up—a custom that symbolized old lives left behind. How was it possible to walk on these rocky grounds without shoes? I wondered. I was reminded of the habit of taking off one's shoes before entering a sanctuary. This simple gesture, one Yahweh demanded of Moses, symbolized the beginning of a new life.

Dimly at first, then more and more clearly, out of the fog trailed the sounds of a bell and monotonous singing. I was mesmerized, pulled up as if on a string. I found a monk sitting on a small mountain shelf amongst mounds of shoe-souls. He did puja, singing his prayers in soft Tibetan, while shaking a bell gently back and forth as snow collected on the rim of his hat. It was the most beautiful sound I had ever heard. Deeply touched by this simplicity and purity, I thought to myself: *If all children could hear such sounds, what world would they create?* Nothing existed beyond this sound, this prayer, the silently falling snow, my breath, and the tears rolling down my cheeks.

As I sat there, our crew passed by. Our luggage was bound to the backs of yaks, heavily built, prehistoric-looking animals with long, thick fur that are domestic to the region and able to travel across rugged, snow-covered terrain. The kitchen gear, pots, and pans towered over the heads of our helpers in baskets they carried on their backs.

We continued climbing, each at our own pace. Any thoughts about the past or the future immediately stopped me in my tracks. I apparently could not afford the energy those thoughts absorbed *and* still keep going. Only one thing at a time!

Finally, with great relief, after many more hours I reached Dolma La. I fell to my knees and prayed in gratitude for this moment, for the good fortune to come here, and for all the events that led up to this, in my and other peoples' lives.

Hundreds of strings of prayer flags had been attached to a tall pole and to the ground, creating a shape like a tepee. Layer upon layer, some flags, bleached to a unified soft gray, dragged on the rocks. Others, newly hung, were still in their bright colors of yellow, red, blue, green, and white, prayers on each of them. They were of such flimsy material that they responded with a flutter to the slightest breeze, leaving no sound at all. Buddhists believe that the wind, moving the flags, sends prayers up to the gods, a thought that made me smile.

I hung up my own flags. They were not just for myself, but for my ancestors, family, and friends. *May my offerings, may this pilgrimage bring peace to my family and to the world.*

Suddenly, the sky tore open, and the sun sliced through the clouds, its rays gradually warming us enough to sit and enjoy a well-deserved rest. A fellow pilgrim in my group read the Kaddish in honor of her Jewish ancestors. Mostly, we sat in silence, perhaps all feeling the same deep sense of elation.

On our way back through Nepal, we trekked through the remote valley of Limi, completely cut off from the outside world by snow at least half the year. During the summer months, the valley is only accessible by several days of hiking on small mountain trails, and only by locals. The Chinese government had forbidden travel to this politically sensitive region in Nepal.

As we entered Halji, one of the three small hamlets in the valley, Tempa approached me.

"Please come quickly," he urged. "This man's daughter is very ill."

The three of us rushed through the narrow alleys between tall stone houses. Looking along the laneways and up, I could see the gray rock of the mountains towering over the village and the buildings. I felt in a lineage with all the doctors, healers, and medicine people who have rushed through streets for centuries to help the sick, and felt connected to something ancient.

Climbing up a narrow wooden ladder on the outside of the house, we passed the stable and came to a landing on the second floor from which we entered the family's living quarters. The only light came from a hole in the ceiling through which the smoke from the small open fire escaped. I was led to a woman in the far corner who was listlessly lying on a mattress. She had given birth to a stillborn baby five days earlier I was told and hadn't stopped bleeding since. Her pulse was barely palpable and indicated anemia. She gave me a pleading, weak smile as I set the acupuncture needles to stop the bleeding. Fortunately, I also had some blood-building herbs to leave with her.

"She has to eat meat," I told her father, unsure if it was available and if he could afford it. Still, I hoped that, with some luck, the acupuncture treatment and the herbs would help her recover.

Tempa and I returned to the courtyard. To my astonishment, our group had left on horses they had hired from the villagers. Our head trekking guide was waiting for Tempa and me. He urged us to follow the group immediately.

But more than a hundred people had gathered outside the gates to the village. Waiting for us, the villagers had brought all their sick family members for healing. Surrounding Tempa and me, in ever widening circles, they shouted and waved to get our attention, gesturing toward the weak and ill. The ones who were closest tapped me on my arms and shoulders insistently.

The sense of tranquility I had felt walking into the village earlier that morning when I had admired the families working the field had been deceiving. Then I only saw the healthy, strong ones. Now I was confronted with what had been hidden; the sick, weak, and decrepit, the toothless and old. What had my fellow travelers been thinking? How could they leave me alone with all of this?

Tempa tried to translate what people were saying: "This little boy hasn't eaten for a whole week," he said, pointing at a young boy lying limply in his father's arms. "This man complains of a terrible headache. The sunlight hurts him so much, he can't work his field," Tempa continued, pointing at a middle-aged man. "This woman has injured her leg with an ax and the wound won't heal."

Looking into these pleading faces, I couldn't bear their pain and the hope that I would help. I didn't know what to do. A panicky feeling crept up my throat, and my eyes began to glaze over. The yelling receded into a throbbing mass of sounds. If there was anything I could do, I'd need many hours, maybe days.

The voice of the head trekking guide trailed through what had become general noise to me:

"These people are okay. This is their life—you can't help them," he shouted with his thick English accent. "You must come now!"

Tempa just watched me silently.

For a moment, I considered changing the course of my life and staying. Everything stood still as I considered the possibility. Wasn't this what a healer would do, stay and heal?

I had no supplies, no translator, as Tempa wouldn't be able to stay with me, and no legal grounds to remain behind. I had no confidence that I'd be able to help. And I knew I'd need the support of another Westerner to survive, emotionally and possibly physically. Staying wasn't a reasonable option. Tearing my eyes away from their faces and justified by my own rationale, I numbly followed the guide.

The man whose daughter I had just treated rushed toward me, handing me his horse to ride. Looking into his eyes, I understood without words that this was his way of thanking me. How beautiful, I thought, remembering how sterile it always felt to receive a check for my services as a health practitioner back home.

But my decision didn't keep me from feeling split apart inside. Had I just missed a most auspicious spiritual calling? All day I found myself in a daze of heightened physical awareness paralleled by a sense of isolation from my surroundings, and strangely, from my own feelings. Was it the right response of a healer to suffering? I kept wondering.

That night our group came together for one of our occasional meetings, a council to share the experiences of our day. My fellow travelers talked about the beauty of the valley and its people, the wonderfully intact monastery, the pleasant rides on horseback. Proudly they showed the objects they had bought from the locals.

When it was my turn to speak, in stark contrast to my comrades' cheer, I sobbed uncontrollably as I talked about my encounters in Halji. The pain I had witnessed, the pleading and hopeful faces that I had turned away from were unbearable. Wrenching my heart, I knew that my encounters in Halji would haunt me for the rest of my life.

A few weeks later I returned home. My experiences in the Himalayas and with the Tibetan people left a powerful imprint. I had learned that putting one foot in front of the other and being present in each step is enough. I continue to find deep solace in this simplicity, and it has freed me from my angst and discontent.

Every now and then in my mind's eye, I see the faces of the Halji people. My heart fills with gratitude and reverence for them. And for the rest of my life I will pray: *May they be well, may they be happy.*

CRACKER JACKS

By: Margaret Combs

It was toward spring, when I was nearly thirteen, that my older sister, Becky Ann, came into my room and made as if we were ordinary girls. She sashayed over to my bed in pink pedal pushers, her hair bound in a riot of curlers, and her skin flushed from Calgon and steam.

"Stop reading," she said, perching her hips on the mattress edge. "*The Sound of Music*'s at two o'clock."

"So?" I flipped the page. I was deep into *Jane Eyre,* with Mr. Rochester draped on my shoulder as he hobbled, swollen-ankled, back to his horse, the two of us drenched in fog and promise.

"So, Mama said she'd drop us off."

A small, astonished yip came from my throat; I clapped my book closed.

It was 1965, and, in our small town of Morrison, Colorado, *The Sound of Music* was on everyone's lips. My friend Nancy had rushed out to opening night and the next day she'd trilled "*Do, a deer . . .*" nearly perfectly to me over the phone. But that was as close as I'd ever dreamed of getting to the film. Julie Andrews was playing a nun, for pity's sake: a heathen. My family was Southern Baptist, just shy of evangelical, and "Catholic" was a strange and hushed word in my home, vaguely sinful, carrying ghosts of idolatry and odd rituals. I knew I wasn't supposed to desire or delight in the happy melody of a nun.

Becky Ann stood and strolled to my closet, sliding the door aside and pondering my wardrobe. At fifteen, she was leggy and fully breasted in a way I'd never be, and already savvy to how rules might bend and sway. I couldn't fathom how she'd gotten our mother to agree.

"Roddy's coming," she said, casually.

"What?" I inhaled. I didn't want to sound like a dog, barking *what what what,* but I felt like one, instinctive and agitated. I stared at the back of her head.

Becky Ann flipped through culottes and home-sewn blouses, wire hooks *screak- screaking* as she zipped past outfits that wouldn't do. As if on cue, a raucous sound burst in the hallway and headed for my door. My little brother, Roddy, was on the run, chasing after his ladybug toy, its whirring wheels and flashing eyeballs thomping along the wall. At eight years old, Roddy wasn't like other boys. He had no friends and spent hours scooting after his robots, quivering with excitement and flapping his hands, his corduroyed legs rigid at the knees, trembling, as if he were an open, buzzing current.

"Do you want to go or not?" Becky Ann said, cocking her hip.

My heart raveled with yeses and nos. As a member of a family with someone not quite right, someone strange in the eyes of the world, I didn't have the right answer. My little brother was a short-circuited boy with darting eyes and a funny way of being. He knew his name and how to spell some words and, in a glancing moment, he appeared like any other boy. But outside our family home, the world was wired with triggers that set him off: lights changing, bodies bumping, horns howling, eyes watching. Each one flipped a time-delay charge beneath his skin, crackling his nerves until he worked up to a moment of implosion, when he'd disintegrate into a fit of flapping, twitching, and frightened barks. What was wrong with him had a string of names, words that felt cottony and crowded in my mouth: autism, aphasia, perceptually handicapped. Only my family seemed to know these words. Whenever we stepped out of our home, another word followed us, sticking to our heels like a mangy cur. *Retarded.*

Becky Ann humphed into the closet. "We'll be fine," she said, thrusting a dotted Swiss blouse and a pair of navy culottes toward me. "Roddy can sit between us. It'll be dark."

I wanted to believe her: that I could be like my friends, like any other teenager. I yearned to feel more of life, to understand how I might fit in. My thoughts slipped to the boy I'd fallen in love with, Wyn Anderson, who only days ago had flashed me a smile in school, letting drop that he was heading to the Cooper that weekend. I thought of how my cheeks had turned hot and my stomach jambly and how I'd moved in a rubbery way down the corridor to home economics class. Word had traveled through currents around the lunchroom that he'd been asking for my last name.

A rosy feeling bloomed in my chest as I pulled my blouse off the hanger. A kind of courage. Becky Ann was right: We'd be fine. The odds were in our favor. Anything that excited Roddy would be nowhere near—no wind, no washing machines, no battery-operated ladybugs with flashy eyeballs that worked him into a froth.

"Besides," she added in my doorway, "it's a musical. Roddy loves rhythm."

Swiftly, I rummaged in my piggy bank and plucked up my comb, lip gloss, and Kleenex. For a moment, I paused at my doorway, breathing in little puffs, and then veered off to the kitchen where I yanked out the Nabisco Grahams, Roddy's favorite. Wrapping a fistful in waxed paper, I tucked the bundle into my pocketbook, dashed out to the car, and dipped under the garage door just as it trundled closed.

For fifty-five minutes, sagebrush and craggy hogbacks blurred past my car window before blending into thick traffic on South Colorado Boulevard. Suddenly, we were pulling into the sweeping entrance of the Cooper Super Cinerama. Fashionably, my curlers, necessary for tomorrow's church, were tucked beneath my blue paisley scarf, a tip from Becky Ann, who'd swiftly allayed my fears that we both looked like hot air balloons.

"No, we look like we're getting ready to go out tonight," she'd countered.

Thrilled, I stepped out onto the curb. *I deserve to be here, at the Cooper, like everyone else*, I thought.

"Take Roddy's hand," Mama shouted out the window. "Keep an eye on him. Make sure he sits between you."

Roddy scooted out and stood furtively beside me. He wore a plaid, collared shirt, tucked into belted shorts, and his pale legs vanished into brown socks and Hush Puppy shoes. He was just tall enough to reach my chin and his cowlick brushed my nose. I took his hand. The crowd, like a swift running current, pulled us forward. Within seconds, the three of us were swept through the glass entrance and deposited into the bustle of the lobby.

Becky Ann pointed to a bench, pressed up against the wall, adjacent to the ladies room.

"Over there," she ordered.

On high alert, we somehow knew our jobs. I herded Roddy to a spot on the bench and looked up to see Becky Ann dive into the waves of people. She called over her shoulder, "I'll get us tickets," and instantly was swallowed up and gone.

A zing of worry circled my stomach, but I batted it away. The hot, tangy smell of buttered popcorn, tangled with sweet stabs of Butterfinger bars,

Jujubes, and black licorice, permeated my nose. The room was charged with energy. Kids my age and older swarmed in clutches of threes and fours, chattering and glancing about the room. I was inside a new world, one thrillingly askew, where anything might happen. Surely, Wyn was here; I knew it. I could feel him.

Roddy twitched, so slight, like the flick of an ear. I murmured, soft-voiced. "It's okay. She'll be back."

"Yaas, Mossie," he said, darkly. His name for me, like many of his words, left out letters that troubled his tongue, like "r" and soft "g." I was supposed to correct him when he did this, but at the moment I didn't care about house rules.

"Becky Ann's bringing Cracker Jacks," I cooed.

Roddy's shoulders bunched around his ears. He pulled on his lip.

"Yaas, Mossie," he muttered.

"And Fresca, too."

"Fresca, too," he repeated, as if he hadn't heard.

"Yes, Fresca."

"Fresca."

Little sparks of anxiety tickled my chest: Roddy's echo was never a good sign; any moment now he might start shouting. Searching for Becky Ann, I scanned the crowd, but her pink-scarfed head was nowhere to be seen. Through the jumble of bodies, a blond-headed blur of curly hair and a turned-up nose caught my eye. Wyn?

I crouched, not at all sure I wanted him to see me. Heart fluttering, I rose stealthily, stepping backwards up onto the bench seat. The sea of heads swelled and swayed, forcing me up on tiptoe, and, in small bursts of desire to see and not see, I hopped up and down on the bench. From the far side of the room, I must have appeared like an agitated fish, leaping above the crowd for a better look and plunging down each time I glimpsed a yellow-headed boy. Once, I dropped so fiercely into a squat, the button of my pedal pushers popped and spun off across the carpet.

I didn't want to bob this way. I wanted to stand still, long enough for Wyn to spot me and flash another smile; but I couldn't. If he came closer, he'd know who I really was: not the girl who'd caught his fancy, but the other one, who lived in an unlucky family with a confounding boy. No one I knew harbored my secret. None of my friends or the families I knew at church. On my best days, I thought this might mean I was inside some tragic story, like Jane Eyre, who made her way forward despite odd family circumstance. But more often, it simply meant I was flawed, deep down, in a place that felt black and bottomless. Floating there was something I believed, and had never spoken of to anyone: God had smote my family.

"Cracker Jacks!" Roddy shouted.

Buckling, I sat down, hard.

"Yes, shhhh, yes, she's bringing some. Don't worry."

"Don't worry, Mossie!"

"Shh-shh-shh, yes. I mean no. It's okay."

Heads swung our way. I yanked out the emergency grahams and pushed one into Roddy's palm. He snatched it and started munching in dinky, angry bites.

Desperately, I looked around, and suddenly, there was Becky Ann careening toward us, weighted down with Frescas in both hands, Cracker Jacks pressed under one armpit, and three peppermint striped straws sticking from her mouth like blow darts.

"Where have you been?" I bounded to my feet.

With a lidded look, she freed up her mouth and handed Roddy his Cracker Jacks.

"Getting the tickets," she said, thrusting a bag of Sugar Babies into my hand. "Here."

"Open it!" Roddy shouted.

I must have looked pale.

"What's the matter?" she asked, frowning.

"Wyn," I whispered, cupping my mouth.

"Uh oh." Rearranging the loot, she reached for Roddy's fingers. "Come on."

We fell into line: Becky Ann in the lead, Roddy shuffling in between, and me bringing up the rear. We scooted into our seats, bookending Roddy on either side. I yanked open his Cracker Jacks, held his wrist, and poured some into his palm; Becky Ann punched a straw through the ice cubes and folded its bendy neck to his mouth until certain he'd taken a sip. For several minutes, we supplied him as his head dipped from straw to sticky corn. At last, the lights dimmed, enveloping us in darkness.

Slithering down, I blew out my lips. My spine loosened, bone by bone, and a cascade of knots released down my legs. No one would see us now. Balancing the box where Roddy could reach, I gratefully turned my eyes to the screen. Within seconds, I was swept into the sky, soaring high over the peaks of Salzburg, and then, with a gentle dive, I descended on the camera's wings to a bare hilltop and a tiny figure, twirling and hatless, who didn't look big enough for the open-throated notes she was flinging into the air.

The hills are alive . . .

The sheer joy stilled me. I sat spellbound, my Sugar Babies suspended at my throat, half torn open. Maria swept me along in a breathless tide of freedom and possibility: a nun tearing around on a mountain top without permission, someone who couldn't bear the rules, the closed rooms or silence of the abbey, so like my house. So like me, she didn't fit her life.

I could have closed my eyes in that moment and needed nothing more; yet, here came the Von Trapp children, high stepping to the pitched bleats of their father's marching whistle. Within seconds, I replaced the players with my own family. Louisa was me, blonde and thirteen, and Liesl, sixteen and dark, was Becky Ann, and also me, since she was falling in love.

For several minutes, I lost track of me: even the wrapper crinkling in my palm, even the bite and pop of sugar on my teeth. Ominously, the Nazis were moving in. So absorbed was I in the dissonant, frightening horns and deep pounding kettle drums that I let out a thin, high squeal when my brother exploded beside me. He vaulted up and out of his seat, whirling his head and flapping his hands, lurching to and fro as if he were a bucking bronco.

I tore my face from the screen. Becky Ann and I shot each other horrified looks and bounded into action, snatching at Roddy's arms and hands. His limbs, whipping around like ropes, slapped my cheek and lip, *whap whap*, sending me sideways.

"Ow!" burst from the chair in front of us, and from all sides came a hissing like missiles through the darkness, "Shhhhh!"

I must have appeared as fitful and feral as my brother. Like a wild forest child unleashed from a pen, or at the very least, an orphan in need of parents who'd do the right thing and yank me out to the car for a good thrashing. But I flailed on, even as I believed that, somewhere in the darkness, Wyn was staring open-mouthed at my large-headed, flapping shadow. I had no choice. I was caught in a situation far beyond my control. Abandoning Becky Ann and Roddy was unthinkable.

I don't know how long the three of us thrashed. It took my sister, taller and stronger, to bring Roddy down into his seat. She caught him in a kind of wrestling hold, folding and clamping him into his chair. As if rehearsed, she and I rasped in unison, "Stop. Stop it now or no more movie!"

Seconds passed, my pulse pounding as my fingers clutched Roddy's arm. Through his shirtsleeve I felt him soften, but I held on anyway, scrunching down, pressing my spine against the seat, cranking my neck so I might catch Becky Ann's eye. Two of my curlers dislodged, and I yanked them out with my free hand, shuddering as the damp curls fingered my neck.

"What now?" I mouthed, but Becky Ann wasn't looking my way.

Through the dim light, I saw her fingers over her mouth. Like me, she'd slid into her seat, her scarf off-kilter. Her fists were bunched to her mouth as if she were trapping something; her shoulders shuddered. When she turned to glance briefly at me, tears glistened on her cheeks.

A thick syrupy pain rose in my chest. I couldn't bear to see her undone. I knew it meant we'd failed at our one chance at normalcy. A noise escaped from her through the darkness, like a sob pushing out between her fingers. I squinted, searching for her face. Then I spotted, in the folded divot of her brow and the crimped corners of her eyes, something that astonished me: mirth.

My hands clapped hard on my mouth, and I dove forward, plunging my head down between my knees. Sputtering, I fought back waves of laughter roaring up from my shoes. It came in pounding swaths, relentless and hard, burning my stomach and escaping from my clamped mouth in a wheezy wailing. I sounded like a moaning child. My nose ran all over my hands. Sugar Babies bounced around my shoes. I wasn't supposed to laugh this way, but I couldn't stop. I didn't want to. Something had cracked open my ribcage, and the pressure inside, held for so long, was bursting with all the force of the earth, blessedly powerful and out of my hands.

How long I heaved, I don't remember, resting between bouts of laughter and then plunging again, wheezing and coughing. Vaguely, I knew Becky Ann was not three feet away, doing exactly the same, and somewhere above me, muffled and far away, I heard the bright notes of birds.

I wouldn't fully understand for two more decades why I hadn't cared to look up and take in the final moments of the happy ending, choosing instead to stay where I was, folded in half, peering at Roddy's socks and Hush-Puppied feet, his pale unmarked shins stilled and relaxed, a confetti of Cracker Jacks littered about his toes. With each new swell of hilarity, rising and receding in my belly, I felt a deeper and fuller sense of relief. I knew finally what I'd known all along. I was not going to pull this off—pretending I could be like everyone else. A door had swung open on invisible hinges and, for the first time, I saw what was inside. I wasn't like other teenagers. I never would be. My life wasn't going to happen that way.

At last, feet and legs began moving all around me, taking people out of the row and up the aisle to the lobby. Lifting my head from my knees, I squinted. Houselights and glances seared the room. I saw Becky Ann two seats away, gazing about, shoulders resting against the seatback. One curler was missing from the side of her head, making her look deformed, as if a divot was missing from her skull. I touched my own head, patting a half moon one way and then another, my fingers dipping into depressions where I, too, had holes.

Far down in front, thick waves of stage curtains began to close, splashing at the midline, a brief flouncing of hem. The theater was nearly empty.

"Toy in there," Roddy said, upending his Cracker Jacks.

TELL ME A STORY

By: Kathy Opie

"Mangia, mangia, eat, eat!" my Nonna exclaimed, scurrying around the wooden kitchen table in her half apron and piling helpings upon our already full plates. When we pointed out the meager three lumps of food on hers, she smiled, dismissed our protests with a "Nevah mind!" and served us more food. A tiny woman at four foot eleven inches and barely ninety pounds, she constantly watched her girlish figure.

But for us she cooked and baked. What a sumptuous feast Nonna prepared when we came to visit. Every two weeks, my mother, stepfather, brothers, and I traveled eighty miles round trip to visit. She'd spend two days baking and preparing platters of sugar-dusted cookies, almond-crusted Italian squares with jam oozing from their sides, and tangy, sweet lemon bars that we'd sneak before and after lunches and dinners. She piled them on fine silver-edged china dishes just for us.

I could never get enough of loving my Nonna, and I knew she felt the same. She'd run down her brick steps as we arrived, engulf my brothers and me in a smothering hug, and cover us with kisses, exclaiming, "Your Nonna loves you!"

My brothers and I had been taken from our mother, Nonna's daughter, when she became so overcome with mental illness and drink that she was no longer able to care for us. I was three when we were placed in foster care for two years while my parents worked through their custody issues.

As an adult, I learned that Nonna was given the chance to take us instead of letting us go to foster homes. But Nonna refused. My older brother and I were sent together to one home, and, after my younger brother was born, he was sent to live in another. I suspect Nonna later felt regret, hearing about the suffering of her grandchildren and daughter, and made a deeply conscious decision to come back into our lives. Shortly after I returned to my mother's home from foster care, Nonna came to visit us at our small apartment in Brookline, Massachusetts, bringing gifts and big smiles. After that, she played a key maternal role in my life.

Nonna taught me to cook and keep a clean house. When it rained outside, we played in her basement playroom. Her hand-braided rug, which covered the bare concrete floor, made a homey area for playing with the toy trucks, games, puzzles, and musty books that had once belonged to my mother and two uncles. These items, calling to be played with and read, sat on lonely old shelves.

We were rarely allowed to set foot inside Nonna's formal living room. Its pearl white carpet, dotted with mahogany and velvet furniture, showcased a baby grand piano with ivory keys that my mother had once played. The smell of Lemon Pledge hung in the air. Heavy, silver white draperies were pulled closed, giving the room a mysterious, dim aura on even the brightest of days.

A portrait of Nonna, painted when she was a young woman, was grandly displayed over the marble mantel. In the painting, she stood in a proud stance, her right hand on her hip, her rich navy jacket open to reveal a soft blue dress and long pearls that set off her blazing red hair and penetrating emerald eyes. As a young child, I could sit and gaze at that portrait for what seemed like hours.

One day when I was six years old, Nonna came up from behind, catching me off guard in the forbidden room. "Do you know who that is?" she asked softly.

"That's you a long time ago," I declared, looking up into Nonna's face. Relieved that she wasn't angry, I added, "You were so pretty!"

"Yes, that was me when I first came to America—all the way from Italy."

"Tell me the story again, Nonna," I begged.

Nonna's stories were a refuge for me. In her stories, I could dream, escape from my troubled family life.

"What was it like coming to America? Were you scared?" I asked, my eyes wide, anticipating Nonna was about to tell me a wonderful tale.

"Ah no, I wasn't afraid. America was new and exciting! And you see, when I first walked off the gangway from the ship, I had my auburn hair. Back then it was very, very long, piled in a big bun," she said, animatedly gesturing toward the top of her head.

"I was something else, with big green eyes, too." Nonna laughed good-naturedly, and then let out a slow sigh. I stared at her short, brassy orange curls and tried to imagine a much younger woman with a different shade of hair.

"A man called out to me from the dock, an artist. He told me I was the most beautiful woman he'd ever seen and that he must paint me!" Nonna gestured toward the mantel. "This portrait won an award, you know. It was called *Woman with Pearls*."

"But why did you come to America?" I wondered aloud, gazing at the painting as if it held answers.

"Well, that is a long story," Nonna chuckled, then walked to the draperies and drew them open. "But since we have some time, I will tell you."

She sat in one of the deep red velvet chairs, and I plopped down at her feet.

"My father's name was Emelio Pierucci. He was a judge, and my lovely mother, Frances, was an opera singer. She would sing in the big halls, the Italian opera houses," Nonna said with pride. She walked over to the coffee table to retrieve a small antique frame that held two sepia cameo portraits and handed them to me.

My great-grandfather looked like a distinguished Italian gentleman with dark skin and hair carefully coiffed in the waved style from the turn of the century. His wife had creamy white skin and long brown hair pulled into a large bun on top of her head. She wore a long white linen dress with tiny beads and lace around the neckline.

"My parents loved to travel on those big ocean liners. They travelled first class, and it was during one of their trips to visit America that my mother gave birth to me!" Nonna paused to watch my reaction.

"Wow, born out on the ocean!" I inhaled sharply, picturing my grandmother's birth. I imagined her mother wearing a long, flowing gown and being attended to by a doctor and servants in her first-class chambers as her precious baby was birthed.

"The most special part was that I was born on international waters, so I was both an Italian and an American citizen." Nonna grinned widely. I realized she enjoyed being special.

"In Italy, we lived in a house by the sea. So I used to swim and play at the beach all day," she continued with a faraway look. "And when I got tired of swimming, I would swing in the hammock on our porch and watch the boats."

"That sounds fun, Nonna. Why did you ever leave?"

"Well, my parents chose a man for me to marry whom I did not love," she explained. "In the olden days back in Italy they called it 'an arranged marriage.'" Her eyes clouded over.

I imagined Nonna as a young woman, crying herself to sleep at night trying to fathom a loveless marriage with an older man. In my mind, he had dark, oily skin and a twisted mustache like the villains in Western movies.

"What did you do?" I exclaimed. Even at such a young age, I understood the difficult decision Nonna had faced. The pain and fear of what it was like to suddenly lose one's family was still fresh in my mind.

"I was both an American and an Italian citizen," Nonna reminded me with a twinkle in her eye. "So when my parents sent me to Pittsburgh to visit family friends one summer, I needed no papers. They thought I was going for just a vacation, but I never returned!"

Her decision to abscond sounded so romantic and impulsive. I was impressed by her fearlessness and a fierce resolve that I'd never seen her express before. I suddenly felt very close to my Nonna and privileged that she would share her secret with me.

"That's how I met your grandfather," Nonna continued. "At a picnic my hosts planned for me when I arrived. He was tall, handsome, and going to become a doctor."

Nonna laughed and played with one of her curls absentmindedly. "We fell in love and got married during his medical school years. Once he finished, we moved to Cape Cod and he started a practice in Wareham."

I vaguely remembered the big white clapboard house with green shutters where my grandfather had his office, a block from downtown Wareham, Massachusetts. My grandfather also kept a small farm nearby where my Nonna built her home and lived after he died.

It was to this house, for one week every summer, that Nonna invited each of her grandchildren for a visit and to buy school clothes. I remember one hot, muggy August day when she and I drove to New Bedford to shop at the fancy department stores. As we stepped inside Filene's, I gazed at the glimmering glass countertops, watched the escalators glide up and down, and felt the air conditioning cooling my sticky skin. *My mother never shops in places like this*, I thought, and suddenly felt self-conscious about my bare legs, scabby knees, and my flip-flops slapping down the aisles.

Pearls in place and purse in hand, Nonna confidently strode to a sales-lady to ask for assistance.

"This is my granddaughter, Kathy, and she needs some back-to-school outfits," Nonna announced. "Now Kathy, go look around and pick out whatever you want."

"Whatever I want?" I grinned, amazed.

It would take me into my forties to learn that my Nonna wasn't as benevolent with her own children as she was with me, that one's view of a beloved family member and the truth can be two very different things.

As I discovered my own passion for storytelling, I decided to learn more about my mother's family history. I started by talking with my mother, but her dementia and hearing loss made it difficult. So I wrote to her brother, my Uncle Royal, with whom I hadn't spoken since Nonna's funeral six years before. I knew he'd researched our family genealogy and had travelled to Italy to visit some of our relatives.

When my phone rang and the caller ID showed a Massachusetts area code, I was excited.

"Royal Davis here. What can I do for you?" His voice was professional, but not unkind.

I noticed that he didn't refer to himself as "Uncle." He seemed to be keeping a distance between us, but why? I tried to assuage him with my next comment.

"I wanted to get some background about my Nonna, and I know that you did genealogy on the family. Did you get my letter?" I waited in anxious anticipation at the significant pause on the other end of the phone.

"Yes, but many of your facts are wrong," he replied, an edge of bitter-ness in his voice. "Also, that woman who was such a positive influence in your life, well that's your reality. Your Nonna was not a very nice woman—she was selfish and abusive. She was a terrible mother and a liar."

His words fell on me like hot oil splattering from a frying pan.

I paused a moment to collect my thoughts. I had heard bits of stories that described Nonna as a vain, volatile woman, but until now I'd been spared the raw emotion and painful truth my uncle unleashed on me. Or perhaps I'd chosen to ignore those stories to keep my childhood memory safe and untarnished.

"She ruined your mother—that's why your mother's the mess she is today!" Royal stated harshly.

"My mother has to take responsibility for her own life and the decisions she made," I bristled. "Nonna didn't force my mother to put my stepfather and his abuse ahead of her own children. Nonna was a good grandmother. If it weren't for her, I wouldn't have survived my childhood. She was one of the few positive adults in my life growing up," I tried to explain as hot tears pricked my eyes. I choked back a sob.

"Well, I didn't know anything about that. I'm sorry. I just didn't know," my uncle repeated. I heard pain and confusion in his voice. Or was it guilt?

"I'm fine now. It's water under the bridge. I just want the truth. I can handle whatever you tell me," I assured him.

But could I? My head was spinning, I felt sick to my stomach, and I wanted to scream. How dare he destroy one of the few pure images of goodness from my past?

My uncle sighed and then began. "What I know is that the family left Genoa, Italy in May of 1908 on the SS Anacona for New York City. Nonna's father and mother and their two children were all travelling together on a business trip."

He paused, then revealed, "Celia Pierucci, their third child, my mother, and your grandmother was born, not on an ocean liner, but in Pittsburgh, Pennsylvania, on March 11, 1909. Her father wasn't a judge—he was a solicitor training to become a lawyer. Her mother was simply a voice teacher. They stayed in America for two years before returning to Italy. I don't know why she told you her mother was an opera singer," Royal said. I noticed how formal and stilted his conversation was and realized he was either keeping emotional distance or enjoyed being an expert. Yet no matter how he spoke, what he said didn't match the stories my Nonna had told me as a child.

It was as if someone had punched me in the gut—I struggled to catch my breath. I detested his version of the past.

"But why would she lie?" I asked.

"Because she's full of crap," Royal laughed. "Like the arranged marriage—that never happened!"

"What?" I exclaimed.

Royal continued, "Mussolini came to power in 1922, and, by 1929, Emelio and Francesca began to fear for their children's safety." He paused again. "Nonna's older siblings were sent to San Paolo in Southeastern Brazil, where the Pieruccis had distant relations. Nonna, because of her American citizenship, was sent to Pittsburgh to live with the family friends her parents had worked with back in 1908–1910."

"But what about meeting her husband at a family friend's picnic?" I interrupted, fearing that everything I'd ever been told was a fabrication.

"You got that part right. At least she didn't lie about him. He was a good man."

My uncle exhaled, and I could feel some of the edge leaving his voice as we continued our conversation. "He was a pre-med student from Hamilton College on summer vacation. They must have fallen in love. He used to take her out sailing."

Royal grew thoughtful. I remembered that his father had died when he was a young boy.

"I still have Nonna's portrait," I said softly. "Do you remember the oil painting, the one painted when she first came to America?"

"That old thing? Talk about the portrait of Dorian Gray!" Royal snapped.

My uncle's jab made me wince. I knew his anger came from a place of past hurts. Our talk left me with many unanswered questions and a lukewarm promise to "keep in touch."

Over the next several weeks, I began to suspect that my grandmother wove a fantasy story about her past because her dream of the perfect life in America never came true. I wondered if my Nonna had escaped an abusive situation in her own past, which would explain why she never returned to Italy.

Was she afraid she'd harm her grandchildren if she agreed to care for them all those years ago? Was sending them to foster care a way to protect them? Perhaps being a part-time grandparent was the most she could offer.

I still don't know what to make of my Nonna's life. Sometimes I wonder what I should believe about her. But what I do know is this: I stand at my kitchen counter some forty years later, wrist deep in shortbread dough. The gummy sweetness sticks to my hands as I work with flour and a small rolling pin to spread it onto a cookie sheet. Nonna's love of baking was a gift she passed down to me. I feel her with me, in the love I share with my own children, the stories I tell them, and in the traditions I share.

Whatever her reasoning, the stories Nonna used to re-create the past and rebuild her life gave me a place to escape, dream, and, ultimately, hope for a better future. Her stories, true or not, saved me.

THE DIPLOMAT'S DAUGHTER

By: Amanda Mander

"**S**o, your dad was a spook?" asked Paul, the American consulate general for Florence, Italy. I hesitated to answer, feeling Paul's smirk hot on my cheeks as I looked down at the translucent green zucchini in my pasta. His voice was smooth as melted bitter chocolate. A sound trained for diplomacy—comforting and insistent at the same time.

My friend Cecilia had made dinner for Paul, her new boyfriend, and me in his Renaissance-era palazzo. It was 1986. I was twenty-five and teaching English with Cecilia to elementary-school children in Italy.

Normally, when my birthplace emerges out of new acquaintance chitter chatter, people say, "How interesting," and the conversation moves on. But Paul knew there was something more to the facts. I was born in Indonesia in 1961 while my father worked as a diplomat there. This was during the height of fears that communism would take over Southeast Asia.

I looked up from my plate, took a deep breath of sweet basil, looked directly at Paul's know-it-all brown eyes and—lied.

"No, my father just worked on cultural exchanges."

My dad was, indeed, a "spook," a CIA agent, when we lived in Indonesia between 1960 and 1964, twenty-five years prior to that dinner. And ever since I was fifteen, when I found out, I continually lied about his CIA involvement to keep his secret. It was so long ago; it wasn't like I would blow his cover. But whenever conversations naturally led to an opportunity to reveal my dad's CIA career, something stopped me and the truth stayed lodged in my throat.

I wasn't sure why I lied at first. Partly it was because I didn't want to experience the inevitable follow-up questions. There would be the superficial ones, such as, "Was he like James Bond?" but then there would be the probing ones like, "What did he do in the CIA?" I simply didn't know how to answer that one and I felt uncomfortable even imagining it. The reason for my lying became even more complicated as I grew older.

I discovered my father's CIA connection accidentally. A family my parents knew from Indonesia moved into the townhouse next to us in Annapolis, Maryland, an hour away from Washington, D.C. They had a teenage daughter like me, and we became fast friends.

Gerald Ford was president the day we sat on the itchy wool carpet in Mary's bedroom, strumming our guitars. America had become a nation of skeptics as a result of the trust betrayed by Richard Nixon. Glancing at me from beneath her brown curls, Mary casually asked, "Do you ever wonder what our dads did in the CIA?"

My guitar string twanged as I gasped, "What?"

Mary's blue eyes widened when she saw the shock on my face.

"You didn't know? It isn't a secret or anything," she said defensively.

But it was a secret at my house. My dad spoke fondly of Indonesia and of being a diplomat there but divulged nothing about being a covert agent. I wasn't politically active at that time and remember just being intrigued that my father would choose that kind of profession. He didn't fit the cultural stereotype of the dashing, sexy spy driving a convertible like James Bond. Instead, he was quiet, mild-mannered—more like John Le Carré's character, George Smiley. He spent all his spare time reading. His clear blue eyes zipped across the pages of foreign-policy newspapers satisfying an insatiable thirst for knowledge about the world. He always dressed immaculately with a tweed jacket and tie—even on the weekends. I thought I was close to him but looking back, it was a closeness that was one-sided. I actually knew very little about his inner life until just before he died.

On a crisp fall afternoon a few days after my visit with Mary, I was ready to confront my dad with my new knowledge of his hidden work. I knocked softly on the open door of his home office. He looked up at me, his crimson tie perfectly tied, his eyes clear and inviting. A fire licked the edges of the stone hearth. The statues on his large oak desk—an elephant balanced on its hind legs and an Indonesian puppet—cast strange shadows on the wall behind him.

"Hello, sweetie," he puffed as a long plume of pipe smoke dissipated in front of his face.

"Hi, Dad." I half-smiled as I sat in the overstuffed armchair across from him. Even at fifteen, this chair enveloped me, making me feel small in his presence.

"I need to ask you something," I continued, feeling my palms grow clammy as I sat on them rigid as a statue—more pillar than girl. "Were you in the CIA with Mary's dad?" I blurted.

My dad puffed some more on his pipe and held my gaze. "Yes, I was," he responded as the fire crackled and spit behind me.

I exhaled my nervousness, not realizing I'd been holding my breath.

"Why don't you talk about it? What did you do in it? What was it like?" My questions came pouring out now that I was over the hurdle of asking.

"I don't talk about it because I took an oath of secrecy when I joined." He still held my gaze. His blue eyes were now clouding over as if he were no longer interested in the conversation.

"But, Mary's family talks about it." I stopped sitting on my hands and unwillingly breathed in the tobacco air around me.

"The oath was for life. It doesn't matter how long ago it was." He looked fleetingly at the fire. "I made a promise and I don't care what other people do with their promises. I keep mine."

In the space of five minutes, his secret had become my own.

Why did I keep my father's profession hidden? After all, I'd inherited my Italian mother's openness—an emotional transparency I couldn't hide. Somehow I expected my father to return this proclivity for sharing experiences. But he avoided any further questions I asked about the CIA by changing the subject, answering with a question, or simply remaining silent. I turned to my more forthcoming mother, who told me she found out about my dad's work when I was a baby. He didn't want her to accidentally mention the late-night visitors to our house who arrived like ghosts without footsteps or voices. Finally, lacking the ability to learn more, I coped with my father's CIA undercover life by burying it deep in my psyche for the remainder of my high-school years. I got so used to saying my dad was a diplomat that I finally believed it.

But then I attended college in the early 1980s, when former spies were writing books about their profession (including my father's former boss and CIA director, William Colby). At my college, I protested a visit by Robert McNamara, secretary of defense during the Vietnam War. When the Iran-Contra debacle exploded across newspapers and television, I developed my own political beliefs and started questioning the role of the CIA. My dad's previous profession was no longer buried. It rose front and center in my consciousness, and I tried again to uncover the details from my father.

On one visit home to Annapolis from college, we sat on our patio surrounded by dogwood trees that filtered the high-afternoon sun. Dad and I were talking about politics, and I found an opening during our conversation to probe further.

"How is it okay for one organization to ignore laws and manipulate other countries?" My eyes locked onto his as I waited for his answer.

He shifted slightly in his chair as a breeze ruffled his wavy jet-black hair, now sprinkled with gray. After a long moment, he answered me.

"To protect our American way of life, we need to understand our enemies and anticipate threats to the freedom we enjoy."

My dad settled back into his chair, likely thinking the conversation was over. Instead, a sense of righteousness energized my body and I stood up to face him. "But how can we decide what is best for other countries? Maybe the communist ideology works better for some places than democracy."

Unbeknownst to me, in that moment, I'd struck at the core of his ideology, the reason for his covert work. My dad sat tall, lips tight, as he replied, "Communism is a form of government that suppresses people in order to maximize power for the few. Every person has the right to participate in their government, to an education, to earn a decent living and to have a good life, regardless of where they live."

I sat back down, struck by the intensity of his voice. It took me a moment to gather the courage to continue, "How far does our country go to achieve these things? Assassinate leaders?" My dad gazed beyond me out to the Chesapeake Bay and remained silent. Raising my voice, I delivered the ultimate question, the one that was the foundation for all others. "How far did *you* go?"

He looked directly at me then and said, "We had to help those who didn't want to lose their country to communism and, yes, we had to bend some rules."

He paused as if gathering the strength to venture into the personal, a land unfamiliar to him, and added, "But I've never done anything in my career in the CIA that I was ashamed of."

A strange relief poured through my limbs as I rested my back on the chair. I needed to hear this assessment from him about his CIA work. His self-judgment somehow made it easier for me to trust him and not know the details.

That day I realized something else about my father and me. We came from two different generations. His was the generation that saw the CIA as heroic, as battling obstacles to freedom, as a force of American good. His America had conquered the evil influence of Hitler and had beat back communism. My generation instead saw the CIA as abusers of power, engaging in sketchy and sometimes illegal activities.

But despite our different perspectives, throughout my early adult life, I avoided revealing my father's previous career. Conflicted, I was motivated by social self-preservation among my peers and more profoundly, I felt protective of my father during the intense societal criticism of the CIA at the time. From our political discussions, I knew he was an intensely patriotic and honorable man. He was my father—kind and supportive. I loved him and couldn't reconcile that he would do any of the illegal activities the media and the public were shouting about. So, I simply stopped asking questions and held onto my own beliefs about his CIA involvement instead.

As I started my own family, and moved across country to California, my relationship with my father floated to the background of my life for a while. During this period, my father suffered many tragedies. My parents divorced, he lost a business he'd built, and, worst of all, he was blinded by a botched cataract operation combined with glaucoma. Life knocked the breath out of him, causing many months of reflection, sadness, and disappointment. He had to rebuild his sense of self, his social life, and even the way he did simple things like laundry or grocery shopping. I expected bitterness to overtake him. Instead, my father rose with a revived spirit and a new openness I'd never experienced from him before.

I called him one night after seeing the film *The Fog of War* in which Robert McNamara acknowledged the mistakes he made during the Vietnam War.

"I was impressed with McNamara's reflections and perspective," I explained to my father as I lay on my family room couch, phone tucked under my chin.

"I'm sorry sweetie, it's hard for me to sympathize with McNamara."

"Oh?" My awareness heightened.

"He had so many opportunities to do the right thing. He refused to listen to me. All those young Americans killed."

By now, I was sitting bolt upright, my heart racing.

"You were advising McNamara?" I stammered.

"Yes, I was in the National Security Council as one of the experts on Vietnamese culture and government. I told him the Vietnam conflict was regional and cultural and that the U.S. should not get involved. I tried to convince him but he wouldn't have it. It was one of the most frustrating experiences of my career."

"Wow, Dad. You were at the center of a pivotal point in our history."

Not only did I feel proud that my dad had fought to keep us out of Vietnam, but I also realized that instead of pointing out facts and circumstances, he'd shared his feelings with me. I was finally getting to know him as a whole person—not just a father, not just as a professional, but also as a man.

As he revealed more about who he was, sidestepping his truth resulted from the respect I had developed for his integrity, his honesty, and his humility. I realized that his work in the CIA wasn't so much a covert activity he wanted to hide from others as a promise he wanted to keep, just as he told me when I was fifteen. By the time he neared the end of his life, I started to defend my dad against others who pressured him to divulge his CIA activities.

In his eighties, my father moved close to Seattle, to be nearby. He started to make new friends, one of whom was a former foreign-service officer, Bill. He and my dad shared a love of politics and world affairs. But, just like Paul, my acquaintance in Italy all those years ago, things didn't add up for Bill. One day as I picked up my dad to help him with his groceries, he had a strange request for me.

"Sweetie, could you do me a favor and Google me?"

"Why, Dad?"

"Bill keeps asking me for details of my time in Indonesia and said he Googled me. I want to know what Google says."

I could feel my skin prickle, a flash of protection shooting up from my core.

"Dad, you don't have to tell anyone anything if you don't want to." My eyes, that he could no longer see, were hyper-focused on the road in front of me. "Bill should respect your privacy."

"It's okay. He means well. He's just curious since he was also in the embassy system."

After dropping him back home, I sat at my home-office computer and Googled my dad for the first time. I found him on a CIA list of personnel, as an author on several declassified White House briefs. He was also mentioned in a presidential paper in which a footnote had his name followed by the job description "on loan from the CIA." With each discovery, the knot in my stomach grew bigger and bigger. The secret we'd kept for thirty-five years was not a secret at all—at least not anymore.

I saw my father the next day for our weekly hot chocolate. In the local Starbucks, I struggled to find a way to tell him of my discoveries. Finally, the words exploded from my mouth, "Dad, your CIA history is on the Internet."

I could see disbelief spread across his face as I described the documents I'd found. He crossed his legs and arms as if protecting himself from my revelations. No longer did he have his usual composed, unflinching, stone expression.

"There was a White House brief on the Internet?" His normally deep, baritone voice shot up an octave.

"Yes," I said as I sought out his soft, wrinkled hand.

"Unbelievable," was all he could say. We sat in silence as we finished our drinks.

While I drove home that afternoon, my windshield wipers whipping back and forth to clear the pouring rain, I imagined the deep betrayal my father must be experiencing. The pride he felt in serving his country and keeping his promise all those years had been reduced to a few lines of digital print. I think in that moment, my father's lifelong belief in America the good started to crack.

It continued to crack with Abu Ghraib, the mishandling of Iraq, and the embarrassment of a Congress that couldn't work together. I don't think he ever got over the surprise of the government's betrayal of his CIA involvement. But in the end, did it matter? He never compromised his integrity, even if the system had.

My father only lived another year after that Internet discovery. But during that time, he seemed to realize the treasure trove of history he embodied. He talked to my kids about Vietnam and his meeting Aung San Suu Kyi, a young fighter for democracy in Burma, now a member of parliament in her country. He spoke at a community gathering about the highest honor bestowed to him by the Laotian government, the Order of the Million Elephants, for his help in shoring up their democratic government so that communism could be held at bay.

Yes, my father was a spook. But, now I understand better the man he was and can more easily accept that the more I dig for details, the more undercover he may go.

STARE-DOWN IN HARVARD YARD

By: John Runyan

Silently, furtively, still half-asleep, we slipped through the gates and archways and into Harvard Yard. Drawn as if to a gathering bonfire, we scuttled along the walkways toward Harvard's center. The police were coming.

Just past 5 o'clock on this already muggy morning of April 9, 1969, University Hall was filled with Vietnam War protesters from various radical Harvard political action groups. They had forcefully taken over and now had been occupying the building for almost three days—bringing nearly all of the university to a halt.

As I approached the central courtyard, I could hear the sound of the policemen's boots. They were marching with a muffled, but growing, cadence that meant that they were almost here.

Angling past this crucible of the protest and looking for a vantage point from which to watch, I saw the lights in University Hall flicker and go out. From within the three-story, gray brick building came a last few cries of protest, then a muffled shout for silence. With hundreds of students gathering around the hall, some in curiosity but most in support for those inside, and dozens more arriving by the moment, the scene was set. Lit only by student-held candles and the reflected light from the windows of adjoining buildings, we could barely see each other.

My heart pounded from the exertion of getting to this part of the yard, so near the action, and my anticipation of the battle to come. I was caught in a familiar political and personal action bind. I had opposed the Vietnam War from the outset when I first learned about it in my high-school years in the mid-60s. But as a traditionally educated, just-trying-to-make-my-own-way ahead, political moderate, I was frightened and alienated by the radical politics and confrontational tactics of Students for a Democratic Society (SDS) and related anti-war groups, especially as they were being led in Cambridge.

SDS was the most radical, outspoken, and prominent national anti-war movement group of that era, with local chapters at many colleges around the nation. I had gone to several large-scale SDS meetings on campus to hear what speakers had to say and to track their intentions for protests at Harvard. I came away educated and sensitized, but also upset and scared. They talked about "getting rid of people" and "blowing away buildings" with a casualness and a fervor that I couldn't stomach. I was also put off by the vehemence of the hatred for "everything American" expressed at those meetings.

At the same time, I had even less interest in joining the jock-led, quasi-right-wing pro-war minority that occasionally poked its head up in resistance to the mainstream sentiment on campus. Instead, I vowed to chart a different course—trying to stay aware of and in touch with what was going on around me, but expressing myself in thoughtful, careful, "within the system" ways. I hated the war and would not have fought in it, but I did not want to give up my college years to a constant running street battle that I then believed could only be won through elections, legislative action, and court rulings.

Looking, as usual, for independent high ground, I found a spot at one end of the very top steps of Widener Library, Harvard's main library, some one hundred yards to the right of the action that was about to engulf University Hall. As I climbed up to this relatively isolated post, these steps seemed different to me. Certainly, they were not as I had seen them as a 16-year-old just three years earlier. I had visited Harvard at that time as a junior in high school, part of my scouting for the right college.

For me at that point in 1966, these steps swept up from Harvard's central social courtyard toward an intellectual Mecca that beckoned me with inspiration and opportunity. They symbolized the significance and promise of the higher education on which I was to embark—just as far from my small-town-in-Ohio upbringing as I could travel. Standing at the bottom of these terraced, granite risers, seeing Harvard for the first time on my own, I was filled with a profound sense of history—already a major interest in my life—and my potential part in it. Looking up at the library's formidable front with its many columns, an inscription etched there in marble stuck in my mind: "Enter to grow in wisdom. Depart to serve better thy country and thy kind." Filled with awe, and, frankly, an egotistical sense of greatness-to-come, I said to myself, "I'm good enough to come here. And do well, too."

Now, nearly halfway through my Harvard years, little did I know that these steps were about to become the ultimate high-rise bleachers for a scene straight out of Kafka. Suddenly, the Cambridge and Massachusetts State Police surged into the yard. First, came three dark blue cars, their lights flashing, but their sirens silent. Then, looking beetle-like and grotesque in their flak vests and helmets with plastic visors, a phalanx of police followed carrying shields and billy clubs. They marched from around Memorial Church and surged up the pathway toward University Hall. Taking up places every three feet, they cordoned off the path and came to armed attention. Then with a deep, guttural roar, five dark blue buses with blackened windows careened into the yard. They churned up deep ruts in the grass (that would serve as a reminder of this day for over a year) and turned toward the hall at a speed that took my breath away and seemed to stun the growing multitude of students milling around the administration building. With a military swiftness and precision, the buses positioned themselves around the hall and came to a stop. There was a momentary pause. I watched as the assembled throng held its collective breath.

And then—bang! The doors of the buses flew open and out charged wave after wave of armed and helmeted police who quickly surrounded the building, pushing students back with their shields and clubs. There was no overt violence in these first few minutes, just the gathering grip of the police force and a few shoving skirmishes.

Suddenly, an intense white spotlight from one of the buses was turned on the left-hand door of University Hall. A small group of police carrying battering rams and tools pushed their way up the steps with the help of a crowd-clearing squad. Wielding their fists and clubs, this unit cleared the student protesters who clogged the steps. Again, they paused just for a moment as a police captain with a bullhorn demanded that those inside come out to be arrested for trespassing and disturbing the peace. Silence. Then two burly policemen moved to the fore and swung their battering rams against the green-painted, solid oak doors. They knocked the historic doors down in less than a minute.

Shouts and cries rang out both from within the building and from the ever-growing crowd of students held at bay in the yard's central space. But as the military operation swung into full gear, a chorus began to rise from the students outside. "Shame! Shame! SHAME!" The thundering voices of hundreds, probably now thousands, of students rang out across the lawn.

More police poured out of the buses and ran up the stairs into University Hall. Again, there was an eerie pause in the midst of the uproar. Then, suddenly, an SDS protester came flying out the door and tumbled onto the landing—thrown there by the police from inside. The police line at the top level of the stairs grabbed him by his hair, picked him up, and threw him down the steps to fellow officers. They seized him again and shoved him, under arrest, into the empty bus waiting at the foot of the stairs.

When I looked back up at the doorway, a solid stream of protesting human beings—supposedly some of the best and brightest students in America—were being pulled, shoved, and thrown out the door and down the steps. Some kicking, screaming, and fighting. Others were tightly tucked in fetal positions to protect themselves from the barrage of fists and clubs that greeted them as they exited the building. The students outside, more agitated than ever but held at bay by lines of police, began to chant, "The whole world is watching . . . the whole world is watching!"

Oh my God! I realized that I been standing riveted by the scene in front of me with my mouth open for what seemed like forever, but was probably only ten minutes or so. *I never thought it would come to this* ran through my mind like a mantra.

I knew that for more than three hundred years no president of Harvard had ever called the police en masse onto campus to deal with any political protest, no matter how severe. Now the police from the city and the state were here, destroying that tradition and relishing their first chance ever to attack the students who set their teeth on edge with their opposition to the war and their long-haired, counter-cultural lifestyles.

Shaking my head, anguished by what I was watching and hearing, I turned away for a moment. Harvard's administrators had said they wanted "civility of discourse" within the university community during this time of conflict. They refused to negotiate with the anti-war protesters because SDS had taken preemptive forceful action by taking over University Hall. I agreed with these academic leaders (and had some empathy for those I knew personally who had been pushed out of their offices) that SDS should not be able to take over the university indefinitely.

However, I thought that Harvard should at least listen, reconsider, and shift away from many of its pro-government and pro-military policies. These policies included conducting war-related research, sponsoring a Reserve Officer Training Corps (ROTC) program for some students, and providing think-tank resources and gatherings for governmental and military officials. In any case, I thought that bringing this army of police onto the campus was completely misguided. As I watched the police oust the building-occupiers, I was nauseated and deeply distressed by the violence that was consuming my college home.

At that moment, for some reason, I happened to look over my shoulder. A shadowy figure in dark clothing, with a flash of white peeking through, caught my eye on top of a building to my right, behind and above me. I wondered who could be on the roof of the house that stood on this opposite corner of the quadrangle from the embattled administration building. I peered back through the hazy darkness and faint light of the approaching dawn. The person was on the president's house, a large brick mansion that loomed over the southeast approach to the yard.

My God! It was Nathan Pusey himself, the sixty-two-year-old president of Harvard, standing in his crimson bathrobe and white-trousered pajamas on the roof of his back porch. He had a pair of binoculars up to his eyes in his right hand, and he was staring intently at the police squadrons carrying out his orders to clear his administration building. Even in the half-light, I thought I could detect his hand shaking slightly and a smirk on his lips.

I couldn't believe it. "What a chicken shit!" I sputtered to myself. "How the hell can he do this? What is he doing hiding in the darkness watching this police invasion like a tin-horn dictator afraid to show his face?"

I shook my fist at him! Even I, who wanted no part of SDS and their vitriol, wanted to wring his neck—this abject tyrant! Against the backdrop of the chaos and chanting behind me, I screamed, "You jerk! You son of a bitch! What are you doing? Stop this! Stop this!"

Though there was absolutely no chance that he could have heard me, somehow I caught his attention. His gaze shifted for a moment and, surprisingly, his binoculars swung in my direction. Standing on this high left-hand corner of the Widener Library steps, I was the person in this scene nearest his perch on the top of his home. I waved my arms, shook my fist, and screamed at him in frustration and outrage.

For a moment our eyes locked. I peered at this slumping figure of a white-haired, haggard old man silhouetted in the shadows by the police spotlights in his backyard; he stared back in telescopic fashion at this athletic-looking young man with a flat-top haircut, clean khakis, and a crimson Harvard sweatshirt, his arms raised and waving wildly.

Neither of us flinched.

And no one else noticed him or me. We were alone in our either-end-of-the-telescope recognition. Left to our solitary perceptions and private projections in the midst of a transformational event the likes of which Harvard had never seen. Wondering what the hell that other person was doing. Just an instant in a fulcrum-like turning point in both of our lives.

I was curious at the time, and later, about what was going through his head. Did he recognize that in losing me—a fairly traditionally inclined Harvard College student and a political moderate—he had lost any chance of being a leader for virtually all of the students at Harvard? Did he realize that his decision to call for this police incursion would, as it turned out, be the end of his career? Was this the way he wanted to be remembered? He seemed so pale, pathetic, and pusillanimous—using a kind of arms-length remote-control approach to send in the police in a time that had passed him by. At the very moment when he was exercising a power that no Harvard president had ever used before (or since), he seemed to me to be helpless, useless, and defeated.

I wonder now exactly what was going through my head at that moment, too. Did I realize that I was at a sharp turning point in my life? Did I sense that I was being firmly pushed off my own moral and political center? Away from Harvard and its tradition-filled values and ways toward a far more personally independent position than I had ever taken before? From that moment on, I always sought leaders who were willing to put themselves on the line in moments of crisis and conflict. I'd seen a perfect "profile in cowardice" from Pusey—and I wanted no more of the lack of courage he was demonstrating.

I did not know then what the longer-term impact on me was to be. Though I had grown up to be a classic Harvard student of whom its conservative leader would have been proud, I did not finish my four years there in that mode. And though I situationally sided with those who opposed Harvard's president that day, I did not enroll in SDS's radical ranks. From that April of 1969 on, I chose to pursue my own third way.

FINDING UNCLE YOSH

By: Wendy Noritake

I didn't know my Uncle Yoshito Noritake. He died in World War II in 1944, eight years before I was born. But in the spring of 2007, as I sat at my computer in the den of my home in West Seattle, he came to me.

I was gazing out the window at the cold dark waters of the Salish Sea when his name, "Yosh," appeared in my mind—like a whisper, a wisp of smoke from a blown-out candle, or fog in a misty dream. I felt he wanted to be known.

It was a familiar feeling, this sensation, a "knowing." It wasn't the first time I'd had this sort of experience. In high school, a teen runaway I'd befriended came to me in a dream saying she was leaving; it was time for her to hit the road. The next morning, at school, I heard she'd drowned in a bathtub during the night. I wasn't shocked or frightened—somehow I knew she needed to go.

Not long after Yosh came to me, I began in earnest to uncover bits of information about him over the Internet. I felt like a detective, deciphering clues in my search for a ghost. What I discovered was a scholarly young man who was in the honor society at Cleveland High School in Seattle. His favorite hobby was Latin, but he also held court in the French Club. Yosh was not only smart, but dashingly handsome with his pouty lips and full head of hair with locks falling forward in his eyes.

In conversations with my dad before he passed away, he talked about his brother and the internment. "When a teacher asked me, 'Isn't Yosh your older brother?'" my dad laughed fondly, "I'd tell them, 'Yes, but you're not getting another honor student with me!'"

Night after night, I pored over World War II and genealogy sites. One evening, in the glow of the screen, I found a large, faded photograph that showed rows of servicemen, standing in light-colored uniforms. Each man wore a standard-issue rectangular cap cocked to the side of his head. This was not just a platoon of soldiers. These men were Nisei, second generation Japanese-Americans, who'd enlisted in the army while their families were held in internment camps surrounded by barbed wire and patrolled by armed guards who had orders to shoot if anyone tried to escape.

In the photo, someone had penciled what looked like a halo around the head of one of the men. The halo, as it turned out, encircled my Uncle Yosh. With a slight smile on his lips, he appeared much leaner than his high-school photo. *How did that halo happen to be there?* I wondered. To me, it confirmed that his spirit, shining so brightly, had somehow found and touched me.

I cropped and enlarged his face so that I could get a closer look. *He looks like my cousin Jeff!* I thought. The facial features were so familiar, like looking into the family gene pool. My dad, uncle, brother, and male cousins all had the same small, baby face, full dark hair, and that pouty mouth. I could discern Yosh with those features from the faces of more than 125 men, even without the halo.

During World War II, the Noritake family was among 120,000 Japanese-Americans living on the West Coast who were forced from their homes and evacuated to internment camps. My dad remembered being rounded up on the Cleveland High School football field with other Japanese-Americans, while their fellow classmates watched with sadness and curiosity from their classroom windows. Yosh, twenty-one years old, had graduated by then, and since jobs were hard to find, he was trucking produce to local stores.

Allowed one suitcase per person, the families first made their way to what was called Camp Harmony—in reality the livestock stalls at the Puyallup Fairgrounds. From there, they were transported by train, windows blackened so they couldn't see where they were going, to the Minidoka Relocation Camp in Jerome, Idaho. There they would spend the next three years in shack-like barracks, sharing space with other families, separated only by sheets hanging on clotheslines.

My dad recalled, "You could see the sky through the cracks in the barrack walls, and, oh, the freezing wind whistled in the winter and brought blinding dust in the summer. Everything was covered in mud or dust."

Dad also said that Yosh enlisted in the U.S. Army despite heavy protest from their father who had already lost his wife and three children a few years earlier. Dad shook his head. "Oh, your grandpa was furious!"

Yosh felt that he was American first, Japanese second, and he wanted to prove he was a loyal American citizen. The vast majority of men in the 442nd Regimental Combat Team felt it was their duty to fight for the United States, and he was no different.

A descendant of adventurers and pioneers, his parents having left their families behind in Japan to seek a new life in America, Uncle Yosh may have enlisted because he yearned to venture beyond the boundaries set for him. He was a scholar and had studied European history, especially the history of England, France, and Italy. He may have dreamed of seeing the historical cities for himself. Volunteering to serve also gave Uncle Yosh the opportunity to leave the prison camp.

I inherited the same passion for pushing past boundaries. Uncle Yosh and I are kindred spirits, and maybe that's why he got in touch with me. Perhaps he sought me to clear up any confusion about where he died. The family believed he was killed in Anzio, Italy, but I was soon to learn otherwise.

Yosh joined the all-Japanese-American 442nd Regimental Combat Team in May 1943 at Camp Shelby, Mississippi. By the end of the war, the 442nd would be recognized as the most highly decorated group in U.S. military history—garnering more than 18,000 medals and citations.

As I considered these many military honors, my thoughts returned to the families these soldiers left behind in the internment camps. How would I feel if the FBI or military forced their way into my home, ransacked drawers and closets, told me that I had three days to get out with one suitcase? There was no time to sell a house or a car or close a business. What must it be like to be dispossessed and sent away even though I'd done nothing wrong and was a U.S. citizen? To be discriminated against, hated, and imprisoned because of the way I looked?

I scrolled through reams of information. Yosh's name appeared in countless lists of deceased Japanese-American Nisei military men from the Minidoka Relocation Camp. In army recruitment papers from Jerome, Idaho, his last address of residence was the internment camp, not Seattle, where he had been born and raised. There were detailed accounts of the days leading to his death. But information about his service and possibly his death were lost in the1980s due to a fire in the Federal Archive in St. Louis, Missouri.

One day during my search, I came across a request: "Looking for students from Cleveland High School." I looked closer. Someone was asking for information about several students, and one of them was Yoshito Noritake. There was an email address. I sent a reply, not knowing if the address was still valid.

The next morning, a response came. "I would like to meet you. Call me."

This was my introduction to Patricia Rosenkranz, a former school-teacher, a graduate of Cleveland High School in the early 50s, and the person who posted the web announcement. "Did you find me because of the forest?" she asked. "Was it my book?"

"I don't know anything about a forest or a book," I replied. "I found your post on the Internet asking for information about my uncle."

Pat, a petite woman with blondish-white hair, greeted me with a warm smile as I arrived at her home. Sitting in her sunroom, we shared stories about the deceased students. She gave me a copy of her book, *Honored Dead, The Story of Cleveland High School's World War II Gold Star Men.*

I opened it and turned to page ninety. There was the handsome young face of Uncle Yosh in his 1940 senior-class photo, a picture I'd never seen. My hands trembled as I held the book. A chapter was devoted to him.

Over the weeks, I had finally been able to piece together what had happened to my uncle. But, somehow, seeing Uncle Yosh commemorated in Pat's book, made the details of his experience come alive for me. Arriving in Italy in May 1944, he fought in major battles through Italy and into France. In October 1944, as the 442nd moved toward Bruyere, France, the days became bleak and harrowing. The 442nd was low on ammunition, medical supplies, and food. And no known army had been able to break through the forests of the Vosges Mountains until then. The weather was wet, frigid, and foggy, dampening the men's spirits.

I couldn't help but think how cold and miserable my uncle and his fellow soldiers must have been. Icy rain turned their breath into clouds, and sometimes their nostril hairs froze. The dampness penetrated to their bones. Mountains, sky, and water could appear as hues of one color—a dark, depressing gray.

Worse yet, I learned that the Germans fought with "tree burst" bombs that savagely pierced the body. The 442nd were bombarded with small-arms fire as they dodged crippling Schu mines. The wind howled through tree limbs and the snapping and cracking of branches kept the men constantly alert, aware that German soldiers might be approaching.

Did Uncle Yosh know that his combat team was on a sacrificial mission to break through a stronghold of Germans who'd trapped the Texas 141st Division's "Lost Battalion"? Did he regret joining the army? Was he afraid? I felt sick imagining my uncle engulfed in war. Had he resolved his differences with Grandpa before he left the camp? Did he miss his family? Did he give up due to sheer exhaustion, hunger, and cold? Did he suffer in death?

Major General Dahlquist, an inexperienced military man, sent the 442nd to rescue the Lost Battalion, who had become trapped due to his errors. Dahlquist shouted to a Nisei soldier who questioned where they were headed, "Go get the Texans out if it takes every damn one of you!"

In the days leading up to the Texas Battalion rescue, the 442nd sacrificed 800 Japanese-American Nisei soldiers to save 211. Uncle Yosh died on October 16, 1944 in the mountains near Bruyere, on one of the worst days of fighting. He was twenty-three years old. I was filled with sorrow knowing what he endured but was glad to have information to give my family.

Later, Pat told me a remarkable story, one that I'd never heard. I was sure no one in my family knew about it, either.

"In 1945, Cleveland High School's vice principal, Ron Imus, went to a land auction with money students and faculty had raised to buy a piece of property," she said. "They wanted to create a memorial to the students who gave their lives during World War II."

Here her voice grew a little shaky. "When the other auctioneers heard Mr. Imus's story, no one bid against him. He bought more than 130 acres of land in the Issaquah/Fall City area for $300 from bake sales and pocket change." Gesturing with her thin arms, she continued. "Deep in the forest—and you have to hike to it—is a large rock with a plaque inscribed with the names of the students who died."

I could imagine the kids selling cupcakes and cookies, washing cars, and asking for donations to remember and honor their fallen classmates.

Over the years, teachers bussed students to the forest to study the flora and fauna, plant trees, and build a pavilion to hold services. But over time, the property fell into disarray.

By the year 2000, school officials wanted to sell the property, which was now worth more than $15 million, so they could use the proceeds to fund other school projects. But alumni, attorneys, and outspoken advocates like Pat, put a stop to the sale.

Determined to save this shrine, Pat and a Cleveland High School teacher directed the students to research each of the fallen soldiers. It was during this time that they posted the web request that I saw in 2007. From their combined research, Pat wrote the book, *Honored Dead*, which captured the essence of each soldier student in his brief life. Their deaths were laid out in chronological order. Their military campaigns spanned the length and breadth of the globe: from the South Pacific to Africa and Europe.

Calling me back from the French battlefields, Pat asked, "Why don't you and your family come to the Memorial Day service next week? We're planning a ceremony complete with honor guards, gun salute, taps, flag folding, a skit by the students, and a walk to the rock."

"I'd be honored," I said, as I pondered what the boulder would look like, how it would feel to walk there, to know that Uncle Yosh's name had been on that rock for sixty-two years, though none of the family knew about it.

"Please bring any of your relatives who might want to come along."

Uncle Yosh's youngest sister, Auntie Pat (Patricia Tatsumi Noritake Uno), was seventy-nine years old that year. We arrived at the forest on a warm, sunny Memorial Day in 2007. The trees that encircled the parking lot—firs, maples, cedar—filled the air with woody scents. The spring sun on the wet cool plants seemed to create a steam that mingled with the aroma of freshly mown grass. As we walked, Auntie Pat talked about her brother.

"When Yosh was in high school," she began, "I was about ten years old, and I asked him what the word 'constitution' meant. He told me that I was an ignoramus. You know, he was the smart big brother, and I was the dumb little sister." Her face broke into a huge grin.

I gazed at my tiny aunt, appreciating her fine bone structure and her lively, deep-set eyes. Her face, barely wrinkled, had won both hearts and beauty pageants in her youth.

We made our way to the clearing, uncertain what to expect, and sat on gray metal folding chairs. Before us, a stage had been set up for the morning's events.

First, there was a flag ceremony, led by men dressed in uniforms that looked like those worn in the First World War. A master of ceremonies stood at the podium and led the students, faculty, alumni, veterans, and families in prayer. I glanced at the assembled group. In their faces, I saw many nationalities who now attend Cleveland High School: Asians, African-Americans, Hispanics, Middle-Easterners, as well as Caucasians. In silence, I prayed for the end of racism, discrimination, and an end to all wars.

"Would the Noritake family please stand?" the speaker asked.

I took my aunt's warm hand. We smiled at each other, grateful to be part of the service.

My eyes filled with tears during the gun salute and taps.

"His body was eventually shipped back to Seattle," my father told me. "But no medals or awards could ever bring him back."

I remembered seeing a photo of Uncle Yosh's funeral. It looked like a family Buddhist service, so I doubt there were any taps or gun salutes—or even words from the military. Behind his coffin, though, a large U.S. flag hung on the wall. The service was Nichiren Buddhist. With incense burning, each participant (priests and parishioners) held a small drum and kept rhythm with a wooden stick. They chanted, *"Namu myoho renge kyo."* ("I awaken to the Buddha nature where our lives and the universe are one.") This funeral service had been part of my family's tradition for more than 450 years.

The service was held in a red brick building, a nondescript Nichiren church that blended into the city. My grandfather established it in Seattle in the early 1900s. To the people who forced my family into concentration camps, Buddhist ceremonies only added to the conviction that Japanese-Americans were definitely different. Foreigners.

Everyone rose after the Cleveland ceremony and began to walk down a recently groomed path. I paused, noticing its unevenness, the twists and turns in the trail. Unsure what was around the next corner, I followed the path down and around trees and shrubs that varied by height and variety. The scent of pine and cut grass filled the air, and I could hear red-winged blackbirds and swallows calling out as we walked in single file, silent. *Could Uncle Yosh hear the birds singing in the trees of the Vosges Mountain forests?* I wondered, *or were they drowned out by artillery fire?*

A large boulder appeared abruptly after a turn in the path. I didn't expect such a huge natural rock to be there. It was as if Paul Bunyan had accidentally dropped a marble, and it seemed out of place. On the north side of the boulder, a brass plaque, about two feet wide and one foot high, was framed on three sides by soft green moss and small strands of ivy. At the top of the plaque, a brass eagle, in relief, clutched a bundle of wheat in its claws. Beneath it were the words: "In Memoriam to Those Honored Dead of Cleveland High School Who Gave Their Lives for the Freedom of Our Country in World War II."

I had reached hallowed ground. I was certain of it. These thirty-two names were real people, young men whose families were forever changed with their passing. I could feel the presence of their souls as I looked in silence at the plaque. A light sheen of pale green moss caressed the names. "Yoshito Noritake" appeared in the third row.

"Uncle Yosh, you've brought me here," I told him silently, my fingers gently touching his name. "I wish I had known you, but I'm glad to have come this far for you."

Both Uncle Yosh and I were just two tiny dots on the long line of our family's history, but somehow we connected, communicated, and experienced healing. In my journey to find Uncle Yosh, I also found myself.

AUTHOR BIOGRAPHIES

Trained as a neuroscientist, **Lizbeth Anne Adams** currently works in medical ethics. Her creative nonfiction has been published in *Memoirs in the Light of Day* and the online magazine *The Motherhood Muse*. She lives near Seattle with her husband.

Meredith Bailey earned an MFA in creative writing. Her fiction has appeared in various journals, including Shark Reef and Em Dash Literary Magazine, where her story was selected for the Editor's Choice Award in fiction. She is currently working on a novel.

Barbara Helen Berger is an artist and writer living on Bainbridge Island. She is the author-illustrator of ten children's books, including *Grandfather Twilight*, and her essays have frequently appeared in *Parabola* magazine. Learn more at www.bhberger.com.

An editor for thirty years, **Marlene Blessing's** winding path has included running a poetry press, working as a features editor for the *Seattle Weekly*, serving as an editorial director for several regional publishing houses, and working as a magazine and book department editor for Interweave, a press dedicated to the art of the handmade. Her anthology, *A Road of Her Own: Women's Journeys in the West*, honors her lifelong love of story and the West.

Susan Bloch is a global leadership coach and the coauthor of four business books including *The Global You* and *How to Manage in a Flat World*. She is also a blogger for *The Huffington Post*. Learn more at www.krwinternational. com.

Margaret Combs is a former National Public Radio reporter and education correspondent for *The Boston Globe*. She is a recipient of both the Associated Press Award for Arts Reporting and the United Press International Award for Best Documentary. Learn more at www.margaretcombs.com.

Laura Bowers Foreman is a writer, teacher, and editor and a recipient of an Honorable Mention Award by *New Millennium Writings*. As both a novelist and nature writer, she has published in various magazines, journals, and anthologies. Learn more at www.laurabowersforeman.com.

Kip Robinson Greenthal founded Seattle Arts & Lectures' award-winning Writers in the Schools program. Now a full-time writer, she has published several short stories in print and online publications, including *Shark Reef*'s anthology, *Currents*. Greenthal has also completed her first novel, *Shoal Water*, set in Nova Scotia.

Mary Matsuda Gruenewald survived the Japanese-American concentration camps of World War II and went on to a successful career as a nurse and administrator. She gives readings from her first book, *Looking Like the Enemy,* and speaks publically about her experiences in the camps. Learn more at www.lookingliketheenemy.com.

A psychotherapist in Seattle, **Donna James** specializes in couples therapy and adult development. She has written professionally on client suicide. James also practices ikebana, the art of Japanese flower arranging, and has published essays about this experience in *Seattle Sogetsu Branch Magazine*.

Catherine Johnson lives, writes, and farms on Vashon Island, Washington. Her essays and poems have appeared in various magazines and anthologies including *Face to Face: Women Writers on Faith, Mysticism, and Awakening* and *Yoga Journal*. Currently, she is working on a memoir.

After a successful twenty-year career in business, **Susan Little** turned to writing. Her book, *Disciple: A Novel of Mary Magdalene*, can be found at www.disciplemary.com and in audio form at Audible.com and Audiobooks.com.

Amanda Mander is a designer, writer, and mother of four. She is the 2013 winner of the Travelers' Tales Solas Gold Award for best love story and is currently collaborating with a visual artist on a book of poems to be published in 2014. Learn more at www.WriterARMander.com.

Clare Hodgson Meeker is an award-winning author of ten published books and more than twenty magazine stories for children. She teaches writing and makes author appearances in schools and conferences throughout Washington State and Oregon. Learn more at www.clare-meeker.com.

Mary Anne Mercer is a faculty member in global health at the University of Washington in Seattle where she focuses on maternal and child health. She also blogs for *The Huffington Post*.

Suzanne Montagne has been published in *Lost Magazine*. She is writing a collection of essays about her thirty years working as a nurse in Seattle.

Wendy Noritake is a periodicals publisher and marketing communications executive. Her stories have appeared in *Lost Magazine* and *About Place Journal*. Currently, she is writing about travels abroad and life on the Salish Sea. Learn more at www.wendynoritake.com.

Kathy Opie has been published in the *Northwest Sarcoma Foundation Newsletter* and the *Go4theGoal Pediatric Cancer Foundation Newsletter*, as well as *Northwest Cable News*. She is currently working on a book for caregivers and writes a blog. Learn more at www.alittlesomethingtochewon.com.

Ursula Popp is an eclectic healer-medicine woman and educator dedicated to all life forms. Her work has been published in *The Sun* magazine and will appear in Sandy Boucher's new book on Kuan Yin to be published by Goddess, Inc. Learn more at www.ursulapopp.com.

Lindsay Pyfer is a senior writer at Microsoft and writes creative nonfiction. Her work has been published in *The Huffington Post* and *Conversations Across Borders*. She lives with her husband near Seattle.

Kimberly Richardson holds a sixth-degree black belt in aikido and a master's degree in psychology. She is the founder of Two Cranes Aikido School and Two Cranes Institute, which provides leadership programs to increase compassion and decrease violent action in our communities. Richardson is the author of the children's book *Gus Learns to Fly*.

John Runyan is a lifelong listener, learner, educator, leadership consultant, and community activist. He began memoir writing and recording material for an audio book in 2004. Runyan lives on Vashon Island with his wife, Merrilee.

Janet McLain Smith is a mom, a published poet, a long-time psychotherapist, and educator. She is the founder of The Mother House Fund (www. motherhousefund.org), a nonprofit supporting local and global efforts to promote life-changing outcomes for mothers and their children.

Elizabeth Van Deventer is an anthropologist turned farmer and writer. Her Virginia farm has been featured in public talks, blogs, and magazines, including *Southern Living* and *Mother Earth News*. She is currently working on a children's book and a memoir.

Tess Williams draws from years as an environmental executive, entrepreneur in the tourism industry, and parent to a special needs child. In addition to being a world traveler, she is a founding member of Friends of the Farms, for whom she produced a cookbook.

6991923R00111

Made in the USA
San Bernardino, CA
19 December 2013